THE ULTIMATE GUIDE TO
BIRDS OF
NORTH AMERICA

THE ULTIMATE GUIDE TO
BIRDS OF NORTH AMERICA

Michael Vanner

Bath · New York · Singapore · Hong Kong · Cologne · Delhi
Melbourne · Amsterdam · Johannesburg · Shenzhen

A Note on the Contents: *The birds in this book are organized according to the order of the families to which they belong. The most primitive birds are at the beginning and the most developed toward the end. Passerines, sometimes known as perching birds, are the most highly evolved species. Many different families of birds are part of the order of passeriformes and about 60 percent of all the world's bird species belong in this category. For this reason, birds are sometimes broadly divided into two groups: passerines and non-passerines. The American Ornithologists' Union (AOU) is a committee of experts who not only standardize the names and classification of birds, but also set the order in which the families appear. This book follows the official AOU list, omitting those birds that are either rare or casual visitors to North America.*

This edition published by Parragon in 2013

Parragon
Chartist House
15-17 Trim Street
Bath BA1 1HA, UK
www.parragon.com

Produced by Atlantic Publishing
Photographs courtesy of Oxford Scientific Films (see page 256 for copyright details)
Text © Parragon Books Ltd 2006

ISBN 978-1-4723-1007-1
Printed in China

CONTENTS

Non-passerines

Introduction	9	Canada Goose	50
Common Loon	16	Snow Goose	51
Pied-billed Grebe	17	Wood Duck	53
Western Grebe	18	Mallard	54
Northern Fulmar	19	Northern Pintail	55
Sooty Shearwater	20	King Eider	56
Wilson's Storm-petrel	21	Tufted Duck	57
White-tailed Tropicbird	23	Canvasback	59
Northern Gannet	24	Common Goldeneye	60
Masked Booby	25	Ruddy Duck	61
American White Pelican	27	Common Merganser	62
Brown Pelican	29	Black Vulture	63
Great Cormorant	31	Turkey Vulture	65
Double-crested Cormorant	33	Northern Harrier	66
Anhinga	35	Sharp-shinned Hawk	67
Magnificent Frigatebird	37	Red-tailed Hawk	69
Great Blue Heron	38	Rough-legged Hawk	70
American Bittern	39	Red-shouldered Hawk	71
Great Egret	41	Osprey	73
White Ibis	43	Golden Eagle	75
Wood Stork	45	Bald Eagle	77
Roseate Spoonbill	47	Crested Caracara	78
Tundra Swan	48	American Kestrel	79
Trumpeter Swan	49	Merlin	80

Prairie Falcon	81	Razorbill	118
Peregrine Falcon	83	Black Guillemot	119
Gray Partridge	84	Atlantic Puffin	121
Blue Grouse	85	Tufted Puffin	122
Sage Grouse	87	Rock Dove	123
Rock Ptarmigan	88	Mourning Dove	124
Ring-necked Pheasant	89	Yellow-billed Cuckoo	125
Wild Turkey	91	Greater Roadrunner	127
Northern Bobwhite	92	Burrowing Owl	129
California Quail	93	Barn Owl	131
American Coot	95	Long-eared Owl	132
Purple Gallinule	97	Short-eared Owl	133
Common Moorhen	98	Great Horned Owl	135
Killdeer	99	Eastern Screech-owl	136
Sandhill Crane	101	Snowy Owl	137
American Oystercatcher	102	Great Gray Owl	139
American Avocet	103	Common Nighthawk	140
Greater Yellowlegs	104	Whip-poor-will	141
Willet	105	Chimney Swift	143
Least Sandpiper	106	Ruby-throated Hummingbird	145
Dunlin	107	Rufous Hummingbird	146
Common Snipe	109	Calliope Hummingbird	147
Parasitic Jaeger	110	Belted Kingfisher	148
Great Black-backed Gull	111	Downy Woodpecker	149
Herring Gull	112	Hairy Woodpecker	151
Ring-billed Gull	113	Red-headed Woodpecker	152
Common Tern	114	Yellow-bellied Sapsucker	153
Black Tern	115	Northern Flicker	154
Black Skimmer	117		

PASSERINES

Least Flycatcher	155	Black-billed Magpie	170
Western Wood-Pewee	156	American Crow	171
Black Phoebe	157	Common Raven	173
Vermilion Flycatcher	159	Horned Lark	174
Eastern Kingbird	160	Purple Martin	175
Loggerhead Shrike	161	Tree Swallow	177
Yellow-throated Vireo	162	Bank Swallow	178
Red-eyed Vireo	163	Barn Swallow	179
Blue Jay	165	Black-capped Chickadee	180
Gray Jay	166	Bushtit	181
Steller's Jay	167	Tufted Titmouse	183
Clark's Nutcracker	169	Red-breasted Nuthatch	185

Brown Creeper	186
House Wren	187
Winter Wren	188
American Dipper	189
Blue-gray Gnatcatcher	190
Ruby-crowned Kinglet	191
Golden-crowned Kinglet	193
Varied Thrush	195
American Robin	197
Hermit Thrush	198
Mountain Bluebird	199
Eastern Bluebird	201
Gray Catbird	202
Northern Mockingbird	203
Brown Thrasher	204
European Starling	205
Cedar Waxwing	207
Bohemian Waxwing	208
Yellow Warbler	209
Blackburnian Warbler	210
Yellow-rumped Warbler	211
Magnolia Warbler	213
Black-and-white Warbler	214
Common Yellowthroat	215
American Redstart	217
Scarlet Tanager	219
Eastern Towhee	220
Chipping Sparrow	221
American Tree Sparrow	222
Savannah Sparrow	223
Fox Sparrow	224
Song Sparrow	225
White-crowned Sparrow	226
White-throated Sparrow	227
Yellow-eyed Junco	229
Dark-eyed Junco	230
Snow Bunting	231
Painted Bunting	233
Indigo Bunting	235
Northern Cardinal	237
Blue Grosbeak	239
Red-winged Blackbird	241
Bobolink	242
Eastern Meadowlark	243
Western Meadowlark	244
Brewer's Blackbird	245
Brown-headed Cowbird	246
Common Grackle	247
Evening Grosbeak	249
Red Crossbill	251
American Goldfinch	252
House Sparrow	253
Index of Common Names	254
Index of Scientific Names	255
Picture Acknowledgments	256

INTRODUCTION

orth America has an abundance of bird life: more than 900 species either breed here, visit regularly or simply drop by occasionally. Being able to identify an individual species is highly satisfying and the pursuit of finding and identifying birds is a great way of getting back in touch with nature. Of course many of the birds that are resident or visit the continent are only found in the remotest of places, some are extremely rare, others may spend most of their time offshore and even very experienced of birders may not have seen them. The birds chosen for this guide are those that are either resident here or are frequent visitors and the selection made is of those that the amateur enthusiast is most likely to encounter.

In order to confidently identify an individual bird, this book contains a number of features designed to help. Each of the major species is clearly illustrated with a color photograph which will initially help with identification. This is supported by a concise description of the main physical features of the bird, its size, and some of the more useful details about its body, wing, or tail shape. Its typical habitat is described, as are any similar species with which the bird in question could be confused. In addition to this, interesting details about the bird's behavior and habits are included since these can be a useful means of identifying a particular species or sub-species. Where relevant for identification purposes, an individual bird's song or call is described, although of course this is difficult to accurately describe in writing. Nesting habits are included, with a brief description of the type of nest, its location, i.e in a tree cavity or hidden on the ground, the typical number of eggs that may be laid, and a general description of those eggs. Details on nesting are by necessity brief and general since many birds will produce more than one brood in a season and it can be difficult to be precise about how many eggs are laid and how long they may take to incubate.

Birds can be spotted at any time of the day, perhaps soaring high in the sky looking for prey, or visiting garden feeders. However, the best times to look for birds are either early in the morning—when they will tend to be most active—or during the early evening. Of course different species are best spotted at certain times of the year, perhaps during their migraton periods when they are more likely to be in any given area, or during their breeding seasons, when the male may be sporting a more easily distinguished plumage. Plumage changes can make identifying particular species more difficult—many birds will change their plumage at least once during the cycle of a year; males are often very different from females; whilst juvenile birds and molting males are often odd-looking. Where this is the case, as much detail as possible has been supplied. It's worth remembering that all birds are individuals and may not exactly match the photographs in the book. It is important therefore to concentrate on the shape and pattern of markings and to use more than one field mark to make an identification.

The size of a bird can be vital. Many species can easily be confused if looking at only their plumage—for instance a black bird seen on open farmland could be a Brown-headed Cowbird, or if large, a Common Grackle. In such an instance size can be the only determining feature. Practise will enable the keen birder to confidently assess the size of species.

North America offers an abundance of different habitats for all forms of wildlife, and understanding the kind of habitat that a bird prefers is a big clue in identifying a species. Many birds will prefer a particular habitat whilst breeding, perhaps dense coniferous woodland, and then choose to relocate to areas where food is in greater supply. Appreciating the importance of a species' habitat is a key way of understanding the importance of conservation—some birds can only thrive in certain conditions and if these are removed then a species can be in danger of dying out.

The range maps that accompany each entry are designed to show when a bird is most likely to be seen in a given area. The same birds are not found everywhere and individual species may also be likely to move from their summer range (usually their breeding season) to a winter one. Many bird species will remain resident in a particular area throughout the yearly cycle and this is also specified on the range map when appropriate. Range maps are particularly important to birders attempting to identify a species that may have a similar relative in another area, for instance the Eastern Meadowlark and the Western Meadowlark, which look almost identical but are separate species with distinct territories.

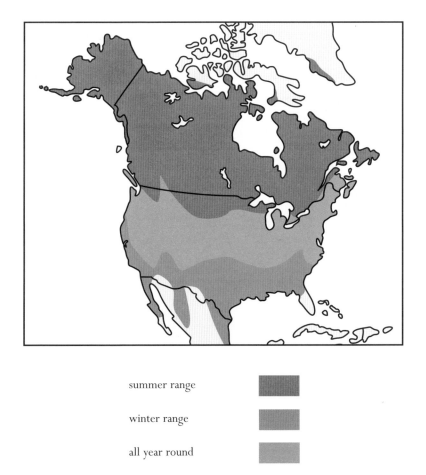

summer range

winter range

all year round

Each of the bird entries in the book shows both the common name and the scientific name. Different species are organized into families that have shared characteristics and whilst some families may only have a few members, others can have many. The first part of the Latin scientific name is the genus, the group within the family that is closely related. The second part refers to the individual bird species. Some birds will have a third part to their name, indicating that they belong to a sub-species, something that isn't always easy to distinguish in the wild. The advantage of Latin names is that they are the same in any language, so birders all over the world can recognize the same bird.

The birds in this book are categorized by the order of the families to which they belong. The most primitive birds are at the beginning and the most developed toward the end. The American Ornithologists' Union (AOU) is a committee of experts who not only standardize the names and classification of birds, but also set the order in which the families appear. This book follows the official AOU list, omitting those birds that are either rare or casual visitors to North America.

Birders should be very aware of their own behavior when out watching. Always bear in mind that the welfare of the bird is crucial and avoid causing any kind of disturbance, particularly when birds are nesting or roosting. Never do anything to compromise a bird's habitat—human intervention can damage and destroy a natural habitat and a number of bird species have been driven to extinction during the past century as a result. Those who wish to encourage birds into their backyard can erect feeders, but these should be kept scrupulously clean in order to prevent the spread of diseases through the bird population.

It is also worth remembering when out observing birds that the rights of landowners and other members of the population should be observed. Never trespass or cause damage to private property, since this is likely to prevent other birders of the future from having the opportunity to delight in nature.

Most birders like to record of their sightings and the best way of doing this is to keep a notebook and include plenty of details—the name of the bird, the date and location of having spotted it and any information about its behavior, habits, and field marks. Such information is particularly important if a rare bird is spotted, particularly if the sighting is to be verified. Rare birds are not spotted only by experts: the informed amateur is just as capable of sighting one if well-prepared.

It can often be worth contacting one of the many local and national organizations that work to preserve the habitats of species under threat, and to protect individual species. They can often provide information on where the best observation places can be found, and will value any information they get in return about unusual sightings. However, don't worry about becoming too involved in how other birders think it should be done; birding should be enjoyable and the best approach is the one that suits you.

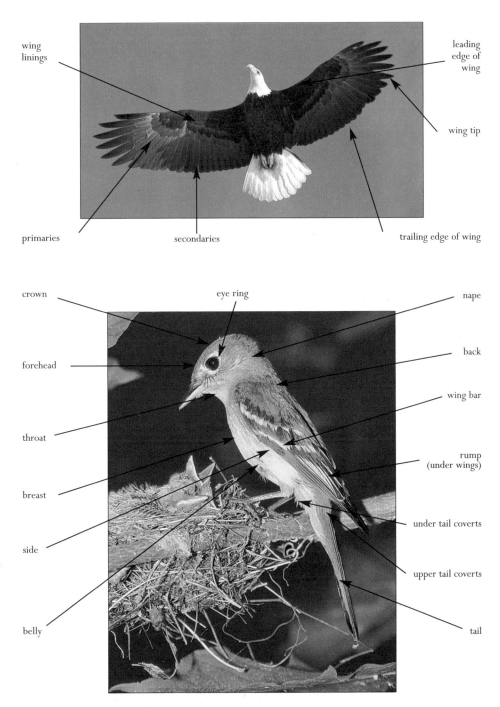

wing linings

leading edge of wing

wing tip

primaries

secondaries

trailing edge of wing

crown

eye ring

nape

forehead

back

wing bar

throat

rump (under wings)

breast

under tail coverts

side

upper tail coverts

belly

tail

THE ULTIMATE GUIDE TO
BIRDS
OF NORTH AMERICA

COMMON LOON (GAVIA IMMER)

SIZE 32 inches
DESCRIPTION Attractive bird with bulky body and strong dark bill. Checker pattern to neck and back in summer. Winter plumage is much duller with a dark back and white throat and underparts. Red eyes, narrow wings, and short, stiff tail feathers
HABITAT Coastal areas and lakes
SIMILAR SPECIES Similar to other loons in winter but with bigger head and feet. In summer is similar to the larger Yellow-billed Loon except for the upturned yellow bill. Common Loon looks more goose-like when flying

The Common Loon is found across North America and Canada in summer although its numbers are beginning to decline as its natural habitat is threatened. It breeds on large lakes and winters on the east or west coast or any ice-free lake. It is well-known for a rather eerie cry which is a method of establishing its territory during the breeding season. Rather ungainly on land, the Common Loon is usually found in the water where it is capable of diving down to a depth 150 feet in search of fish, staying under water for up to one minute. The juvenile birds are similar in color to the adult's winter plumage but with an additional white scallop-pattern on the scapulars.

(PODILYMBUS PODICEPS) PIED-BILLED GREBE

The Pied-billed Grebe is common across North America although those in the north may travel southward in the winter to find lakes free from ice. It is a common but solitary bird that spends most of its time in the water feeding on fish, insects, and crustaceans. It is rarely seen in flight or on land and if threatened it will sink below the surface of the water to hide. Its nest is constructed in the water to create a floating raft which is then anchored to other water plants. The female lays between 2 and 10 eggs that are incubated by both parents for 23–27 days. The chicks leave the nest within an hour of hatching but are protected by the parents for 1 or 2 months, often riding on their backs.

SIZE 13½ inches
DESCRIPTION Remote ponds, marshes, sluggish streams, lakes
HABITAT Small waterbird with dull brown plumage and a short, blunt beak. In summer the throat is black and the bill encircled with a black band, hence its name
SIMILAR SPECIES Other grebes have thinner bills and different plumage. Black ring on bill in summer makes it quite distinctive

WESTERN GREBE (AECHMOPHORUS OCCIDENTALIS)

SIZE 25 inches

DESCRIPTION A large, long-necked bird with a long, thin, yellow beak and red eyes. Plumage is black above and white below with the feet set far back on the body

HABITAT Freshwater lakes and inshore coastal areas

SIMILAR SPECIES Very similar to Clark's Grebe but the black cap on the Western Grebe extends below the eye and Clark's grebe has a bright yellow bill. Similar to loons in winter but with longer neck and bill

The Western Grebe is renowned for its unique courting display when the two birds race across water to dive and rear up in front of each other, often with several hundred pairs displaying at the same time. The birds nest on a platform of plants anchored to other vegetation where 3–8 eggs are laid and incubated for 3–4 weeks by both parents. Both will feed the chicks and dive underwater to get past other nesting pairs who will defend their territory. The Western Grebe eats fish, insects, and small crustaceans. It spends summers on western lakes and then winters in sheltered bays or open inland water.

(FULMARUS GLACIALIS) NORTHERN FULMAR

This medium-sized bird spends most of its life at sea, only coming into land to nest on the cliffs along the Arctic coastline and the northern islands. A solitary egg is laid in any convenient depression where the parents share the task of the 50-day incubation period. The chicks are fed regurgitated food for about 7 weeks before flying. The Fulmar feeds on fish, squid, and shrimp, happily eating refuse thrown over the sides of fishing boats. It drinks seawater as the prominent nostrils can work with special glands to filter out the excess salt. The Fulmar has a unique defensive mechanism by which it can regurgitate a very unpleasant smelling oil from its stomach and accurately squirt it all over its attacker.

SIZE 19 inches (wingspan 42 inches)

DESCRIPTION Rounded yellow bill with prominent tubular nostrils on top. Gray and white plumage

HABITAT Offshore and coastal cliffs in the northern islands and Arctic coast

SIMILAR SPECIES Looks very similar to some gulls but has longer wings and a different flight pattern. Unlike the steady flap that gulls make, the Fulmar will produce rapid wingbeats before holding the wings stiffly and outstretched as it glides over the water. The distinctive nostrils can be seen at close range

SOOTY SHEARWATER
(PUFFINUS GRISEUS)

SIZE 18 inches (wingspan 41 inches)

DESCRIPTION Sooty-gray plumage with narrow wings and thin, dark bill. Male and female are alike.

HABITAT Offshore in the Pacific and Atlantic Ocean

SIMILAR SPECIES The Short-tailed Shearwater is similar in color but with a smaller bill and rounder head. The Pink-footed Shearwater again is similar in color but has a pink bill with a black tip and white underparts

In the summer millions of these birds can be seen off the Pacific and Atlantic coasts forming enormous flocks. The Sooty Shearwater eats small fish and crustaceans and can be observed gliding near the surface of the water searching for food. It is capable of diving up to 60 yards into the water but more commonly takes from the surface, often following whales then catching the fish disturbed by them. It is a long-distance migrant and will return to the breeding grounds in November, which are situated on isolated islands in the Southern Hemisphere. To help it travel these great distances the sooty shearwater is able to pick up and ride on thermal currents. It nests in burrows, in large colonies, and returns to the nest at night in order to avoid predators.

WILSON'S STORM-PETREL
(OCEANITES OCEANICUS)

This species is mainly be seen from the Atlantic coast in the summer months but migrates to islands in the Southern Hemisphere to breed. It nests on rocky crevices or in burrows where a single egg is laid, incubated and the chick is later fed by both parents. It is nocturnal during this time and is frequently preyed on by skuas and gulls and can sometimes be trapped by heavy snowfall. Wilson's Storm-petrel can only manage a short shuffle when walking. It feeds on small fish and plankton taken from the surface of the water, pattering its feet on the surface as it feeds. It will also take refuse from ships and has been known to feed on the oil from carcasses.

SIZE 7 inches

DESCRIPTION Has dark plumage with a square tail. The feet extend beyond the tail in flight and a broad white band can be seen on the rump. Yellow webbed feet

HABITAT Offshore. Very common off the Atlantic coast between May and September and occasionally seen off the Gulf coast

SIMILAR SPECIES Very similar to Leach's Storm-petrol but Leach's has a forked tail and more sharply angled wings. Wilson's shows short fluttering wingbeats in flight whereas Leach's fly with much deeper wingbeats

WHITE-TAILED TROPICBIRD
(PHAETHON LEPTURUS)

During their courtship display the pair of White-tailed Tropicbirds fly in parallel with the tail streamers from the bird above turned toward its mate before they fly together in shallow glides. It does not begin breeding until it reaches four years of age, nesting on tropical islands where a single egg is laid in a rocky crevice or tree cavity. The grayish-speckled egg is incubated by both parents for around 40 days. The chick is fed with regurgitated food and flies at about 10 weeks. A solitary feeder, the White-tailed Tropicbird folds its wings before plunging into the water to capture fish and squid, and eats the prey before resuming the flight. Juveniles have a barred back and lack the distinctive wing stripe.

SIZE 30 inches (including tail streamers)
DESCRIPTION White plumage with long tail streamers. Wings have black tips and a black stripe across the upper wings. Dark eye patch and yellow/orange bill
HABITAT Offshore. A tropical seabird that is common in Bermuda but only occasionally visits North America
SIMILAR SPECIES Red-billed Tropicbird is similar in color but has a red bill and does not have the black stripe on the upper wing. It is also larger

NORTHERN GANNET (MORUS BASSANUS)

SIZE 37 inches (wingspan 72 inches)

DESCRIPTION White plumage with black wing tips. Light bluish bill. During breeding, head and neck are tinged with yellow

HABITAT Offshore in the North Atlantic. Nests on cliffs or small rocky islands

SIMILAR SPECIES In their first year these birds are very similar to immature Masked Boobies. The adult is similar to the Masked Booby but is bigger with less black on the wing and a white tail

The Northern Gannet is renowned for being an amazing diver, plunging into the ocean at very high speeds and reaching a depth of 100 feet. It tends to prey on small fish that swim near the surface. This bird nests in huge overcrowded colonies on rocky cliffs and islands around the Gulf of St. Lawrence but can be seen in the Gulf of Mexico in winter. Pairs remain together for several seasons and can be seen performing complicated greeting rituals at the nest as they stretch their necks upward, tapping their bills together. The single egg is incubated by both parents and the juvenile is gray-brown with white speckles that gradually increase until adult plumage is reached at the age of 3–4 years.

(SULA DACTYLATRA) MASKED BOOBY

A tropical bird that can be seen in the Gulf of Mexico or from the southern Atlantic coast in the summer. It nests in large colonies where 1 or 2 eggs will be laid in a shallow depression. Both parents incubate the eggs using their webbed feet to warm them. Chicks hatch after about 43 days and fledge at just over 3 months, staying with the parents for a further month or two. Males will only mate with one female. If 2 eggs are laid, there is often a gap of several days between hatching and when the second chick finally appears it will usually be forced out of the nest by the first-born and probably die. Boobies dive from a great height to catch fish.

SIZE 32 inches (wingspan 62 inches)
DESCRIPTION Tropical seabird with white plumage and a black mask. Large pointed yellow bill and black tail
HABITAT Offshore
SIMILAR SPECIES Mature bird is similar to Northern Gannet but has more black on wings, a black tail, and yellow bill. Immature birds are similar to Northern Gannets in their first-year plumage

AMERICAN WHITE PELICAN
(PELECANUS ERYTHRORHYNCHOS)

This enormous bird is very graceful in flight with long powerful wing strokes. It can be seen in various parts of North America at different times of the year and nests in large flocks on islands in freshwater lakes. Two or three eggs are incubated by both parents but the chicks have no feathers when they hatch so have to be protected from the sun by the parents. The American White Pelican catches more than 4 pounds of fish a day by scooping up the catch in its large bill as it swims along. The bill and throat pouch can hold nearly 3 gallons of water which is twice the capacity of its stomach. It is protected by the Migratory Bird Treaty of 1972.

SIZE 62 inches (wingspan 108 inches)
DESCRIPTION Very large waterbird with large pouched yellow bill. White plumage with black on edge of wings
HABITAT Large lakes and seawater
SIMILAR SPECIES In flight the wing pattern may look similar to the Wood Stork but otherwise this bird is quite unique with its huge yellow bill

BROWN PELICAN
(PELECANUS OCCIDENTALIS)

The Brown Pelican is a seabird that can be seen off the Atlantic and Pacific coasts in the south. It lives in large flocks and the male will choose a nesting site then attract the female with a display using head movements. He then brings her sticks and grass which she weaves into a nest. Both parents incubate the 2–3 eggs by warming them with their webbed feet. The eggs hatch after one month and the chicks are fed regurgitated food that is initially left in the nest but then fed directly from the parent. The adult feeds by plunging into the sea to grab fish then surfacing and tossing its catch into the air swallowing it head first.

SIZE 50 inches (wingspan 84 inches)
DESCRIPTION Very large waterbird with gray-brown plumage, a large gray pouched bill, and white head
HABITAT Seawater
SIMILAR SPECIES The shape and coloring of this bird make it unmistakable

GREAT CORMORANT
(PHALACROCORAX CARBO)

The Great Cormorant can be seen off the coast of northeastern North America. It lives in huge colonies often numbering thousands of birds and builds its nest from seaweed and sticks on rocky cliffs in which 4–5 eggs are laid. Both adults incubate the eggs for around 30 days and the chicks are then fed from regurgitated food, remaining in the nest for about 7–8 weeks. Juveniles are brown with a darker back and white belly and a dull brown throat patch. The adult bird feeds on fish which it catches by diving down from the surface of the water. It can sometimes be observed in the water submerged up to its neck or standing on rocks with its wings outstretched to dry them.

SIZE 36 inches (wingspan 63 inches)
DESCRIPTION Hook-tipped bill with black plumage and large white band on throat. In the breeding season white patches can be seen on the thighs. All four toes are webbed to aid swimming
HABITAT Seawater, rocky coasts, and bays
SIMILAR SPECIES Similar to the Double-crested Cormorant which has the same colored plumage but is smaller and has an orange throat patch in the breeding season without the white thigh patches

DOUBLE-CRESTED CORMORANT
(PHALACROCORAX AURITUS)

This is the most common cormorant found in North America, and it is frequently found inland. It nests in tall trees or on cliffs or on the ground on an island as long as it is near deep water. Its nest is made from sticks and seaweed with 2–9 eggs incubated by both parents for about 25 days. Juvenile birds have brownish plumage with lighter breasts and darker backs. Adults develop tufts to the head in the breeding season which are black in the southeast and whitish in the north and west. It feeds on fish, diving and swimming underwater to catch them. The Double-crested Cormorant flies in long lines or "V" formations and a slight kink in the neck can be seen when it is in the air.

SIZE 32 inches (wingspan 52 inches)
DESCRIPTION Black plumage with an orange throat that extends around the beak and in front of the eye. Hook-tipped bill that points upwards when swimming. Small tufts appear on the sides of head in the breeding season
HABITAT Rivers, inland lakes, and seawater
SIMILAR SPECIES Similar in color to the Great Cormorant which is larger and has a lemon-yellow throat patch and white patches on its sides in the breeding season

ANHINGA
(ANHINGA ANHINGA)

Being tropical this bird is only found in the southern swamps of North America. It lives in colonies siting its nest about 40 feet from the ground. Between 1 and 5 eggs are laid and then incubated by both adults for a period of 25–28 days. A juvenile has a buff head and neck and less white on the wings than the adult of the species but in its third winter the male's neck and head become black. Swimming with only the head and neck above the water, it uses the sharp bill to spear fish, frogs, and small crustaceans before tossing them into the air so they can be swallowed head first. It can often be seen standing on rocks or twigs, holding its wings out to dry.

SIZE 35 inches (wingspan 45 inches)
DESCRIPTION A tropical bird with black plumage and white streaks and spots on wings and upper back. Female has buff-colored neck. Swims with only head and neck protruding from water
HABITAT Swampland
SIMILAR SPECIES Similar to a cormorant but has a thin narrow bill and distinctive markings on the wings and a fan-shaped tail

MAGNIFICENT FRIGATEBIRD
(FREGATA MAGNIFICENS)

This bird builds a flimsy nest in bushes or on the ground, laying 1 or 2 eggs which are then incubated by both parents for about 50 days. Both adults feed the chicks for some 7 weeks but they remain in the nest until about 5 months old, with the parents still occasionally providing food. The adult feeds on fish, squid, and crustaceans by swooping down to the water surface, but it will also steal from other birds after chasing them and forcing them to regurgitate their catch. It can be found along the Gulf of Mexico and along the Florida coast, normally remaining out at sea. The Magnificent Frigatebird does not rest on the water, preferring to perch on isolated sea cliffs.

SIZE 40 inches (wingspan 90 inches)
DESCRIPTION A tropical seabird with a long hooked bill and black plumage. A deep fork in the tail and long, narrow wings. The male has an orange-red throat pouch that can sometimes be inflated when he displays. The female is more blackish-brown in color with a white chest
HABITAT Offshore
SIMILAR SPECIES Shape and coloring make this bird quite distinct

GREAT BLUE HERON (ARDEA HERODIAS)

SIZE 46 inches (wingspan 72 inches)

DESCRIPTION A large wading bird with long legs and a long neck. Plumage is blue-gray and the white head has a black stripe going across the eye and ending with black plumes at the back of the head. Heavy yellow bill. Gray plumes appear on the chest in the breeding season

HABITAT Still water, wetlands, and salt marshes

SIMILAR SPECIES The Great White Heron found in Florida is an all-white version of this bird. The Sandhill Crane is similar to the Great Blue in size and coloring but has a shorter neck and a different body shape

This heron builds its nest 100 feet from the ground in tall trees or cliffs. The 3–7 eggs produced are incubated by both parents for a month and the chicks leave the nest after 8 weeks. The juvenile is a more gray-brown color and the plumes are absent. When feeding it is able to stand motionless in the water for long periods of time before spearing the prey using its long bill like a pair of scissors. It feeds on fish, frogs, mice, and birds. Although it nests in colonies it is quite a solitary bird and can often be seen flying alone with the characteristic head and neck folded back. It is the largest and most common heron found in North America.

(BOTAURUS LENTIGINOSUS) AMERICAN BITTERN

A very common bird across North America, this bittern is not often seen due to the marshy areas where it lives and the ability to camouflage itself. It nests in isolated places with the female building the nest and the male defending the territory. Two or three eggs are incubated by the female for 29 days and the young leave after 6–7 weeks. Its spring song sounds like a sledgehammer striking a stake, a sound it produces by swallowing air, swelling its throat, then expelling the air by constricting the throat. If alarmed it will freeze motionless with its bill pointed upward to blend in with its surroundings. The American Bittern feeds on fish, small eels, frogs, and insects.

SIZE 28 inches (wingspan 42 inches)

DESCRIPTION Brown and white striped plumage, white throat, and pointed wings with black tips. Yellowish bill

HABITAT Marshes, bogs, swamps, and grassy shores

SIMILAR SPECIES Juvenile bird is similar to the juvenile Night-heron but is larger and has a longer bill. In flight the wingbeats are faster

GREAT EGRET
(ARDEA ALBA)

The population of Great Egrets was much diminished in the 19th century by hunters killing them for their beautiful feathers. Though it is the most widespread egret in North America it is not out of danger today, with drainage of wetlands restricting available habitats. The Great Egret can be seen elegantly walking in shallow water, stalking fish, frogs, and water snakes; it also eats insects. A sociable bird, it is a colonial nester, and Great Egret colonies can be large. Nests are generally built in trees but may be found in reeds, and are sturdy, reusable platforms constructed with sticks. Here 3–5 eggs are laid; both adult birds incubate the clutch for 23–36 days, and the chicks stay in the nest for a further 6–7 weeks. Juvenile birds are white, but not of such an almost luminous brightness as adults; they have no plumes.

Size 39 inches (wingspan 51 inches)
Description Large, long neck and legs; white with black legs; long, thin yellow bill; breeding bird has long plumes extending from its back to beyond the tail
Habitat Lakes, marshes, and wetlands
Similar Species Most other white herons are smaller; black legs distinguish it from the all-white variety of Great Blue Heron

WHITE IBIS
(EUDOCIMUS ALBUS)

The White Ibis is a sociable bird that lives in large colonies nesting in reeds or trees. Two to five eggs are laid that are then incubated for 21–23 days and the chicks fly after 4–5 weeks. The adults feed in groups in shallow water using their long bills to catch aquatic invertebrates and fish. The juveniles are brown with a white belly and an orange face and bill with dull brown legs. It is closely related to the Scarlet Ibis that was introduced into the country and inter-breeding has led to birds with varying pink and scarlet plumage. This ibis is common in the wetlands on the southern coasts and has bred as far north as Virginia.

Size 25 inches (wingspan 38 inches)
Description Wading bird with long neck and white plumage with black feathers on outer primary wing tips. Long reddish-pink curved bill and face. Long red legs and feet
Habitat Swamps, mangroves, and coastal salt marshes
Similar Species The immature bird resembles the Glossy Ibis and White-faced Ibis but has a white belly

WOOD STORK
(MYCTERIA AMERICANA)

These birds nest in large colonies, building flimsy structures in tall trees. After 3–4 eggs are laid they are incubated by both parents for about a month with the young leaving the nest after about 50 days. The juveniles are very similar to the adults but with gray-brown feathers on the neck and a yellow bill. Unlike their mainly silent parents the young are incredibly noisy, producing a whole range of sounds. The Wood Stork is native to North America and can be seen in Florida all year, spreading southwest in the summer. It feeds in shallow water on fish, frogs, reptiles, and insects using their long down-curved bills. Recently their population has become endangered as some of their habitats have been drained.

SIZE 40 inches (wingspan 61 inches)
DESCRIPTION Large white wading bird with blackish naked head and neck and a long, bare-skinned, curved bill. Heavy tapering black flight and tail feathers
HABITAT Shallow freshwater, swamps, and marshy meadows
SIMILAR SPECIES Resembles the American White Pelican in flight but flies with head straight out rather than tucked back and has more black on wings

ROSEATE SPOONBILL
(AJAIA AJAJA)

These birds exhibit an elaborate courtship with the clapping of bills and flying displays. They mate for life and are very sociable, living in small colonies, flying and feeding together. The nests are usually sited in trees, reeds, or bushes with 2–3 eggs incubated for 22–23 days. The young fledge after 5–6 weeks. Immature birds have yellow eyes and a yellowish bill and white or very pale pink plumage. The spoon-shaped bill of this bird is used by partly opening it while moving backward and forward in shallow water to catch fish, aquatic invertebrates, and small crustaceans. The bird was once hunted for its feathers which were used in the millinery trade but its numbers have since recovered. It is found around the Gulf of Mexico and the southwest.

Size 32 inches (wingspan 50 inches)
Description Large wading bird with pink and white plumage. Long neck and spoon-shaped bill that is gray with dark-gray mottling. Long pink legs, dark feet, and bare greenish-colored head with red eyes
Habitat Shallow lagoons, mangrove swamps, coastal islands, and mudflats
Similar Species Resembles the Flamingo in size and color but with a distinctive spoon-shaped bill

TUNDRA SWAN (CYGNUS COLUMBIANUS)

SIZE 52 inches (wingspan 80 inches)
DESCRIPTION Large, long neck; white with black bill, bright yellow spot in front of eye; neck generally held straight
HABITAT Shallow ponds, lakes, marshes, and rivers
SIMILAR SPECIES Trumpeter Swan has longer bill and is larger, as is the Mute Swan, which has an orange bill

As its name suggests, the Tundra Swan – formerly known as the Whistling Swan because of its musical voice – is principally found on the Arctic tundra. It is the smallest North American swan, spending summers in the north but migrating southward in winter. It is often seen in flocks and has a tendency to return to the same place year after year. Most Tundra Swans feed on both land and water; they eat small mollusks, invertebrates, and aquatic plants. Breeding takes place on the tundra, where it builds a large mound of grass and leaves as its nest; the 2–7 eggs are incubated by the female for an average of 32 days. A young Tundra Swan has gray-brown plumage and appears rather dull; its bill is pink. It develops its adult coloration more quickly than do juveniles of other swan species.

(CYGNUS BUCCINATOR) TRUMPETER SWAN

This species almost died out at the beginning of the 20th century as it was hunted for its eggs, down, and skin. It then became a protected species and since then the numbers have increased. It is found in the northwest but is also being introduced further east. It breeds near water, finding plant material to construct the nest. The female lays and incubates 2–13 eggs which take about 33 days to hatch. The cygnets are able to leave the nest soon after but stay with the parents until the following spring. The juvenile has dull gray-brown plumage and a pinkish bill. The Trumpeter Swan feeds on insects and aquatic plants using its long neck to reach them.

SIZE 60 inches (wingspan 96 inches)
DESCRIPTION Large waterbird with a long, straight neck, white plumage, and a black, straight bill. Black facial skin that forms a "V" on the forehead
HABITAT Rivers and wooded ponds
SIMILAR SPECIES Resembles Tundra Swan but has a longer bill with no yellow coloring and is bigger. Juvenile is similar to juvenile Mute Swan but holds neck straight rather than in an S-shape

CANADA GOOSE (BRANTA CANADENSIS)

SIZE 25–45 inches (wingspan 48–72 inches)

DESCRIPTION Dark plumage on back and tail with white undertail. Head and neck are black with white chin strap. In flight U-shaped rump band and dark wings can be seen

HABITAT Ponds, lakes, bays, estuaries, grasslands, and marshes

SIMILAR SPECIES Small birds are similar to the Brant but the Canada Goose has the distinctive chin strap

The Canada Goose is found all over America at varying times of the year and when migrating will fly in a V-formation, stopping frequently to feed. It eats grass, grain, small aquatic animals, and plants. The population is currently on the increase and the size of the birds varies quite considerably, with those in the north tending to be smaller. In the breeding season the male becomes very aggressive as he defends his territory, even attacking larger birds if necessary. The nest is constructed from plant matter and down in fairly open areas near water. The female lays and incubates 2–12 white eggs that hatch after 25–30 days. The downy juveniles soon leave the nest but stay with the parents until the following spring.

(CHEN CAERULESCENS) SNOW GOOSE

The Snow Goose breeds on Arctic tundra and then migrates in very large flocks. It is very common in parts of the south in winter. It nests in colonies near water lining a shallow depression and laying 3–8 eggs. The young hatch after 22–25 days and will remain with the parents until the following spring. These birds feed on grain, insects, and aquatic plants and can often be seen grazing in fields in the winter. There is another color variation previously known as the Blue Goose which has a brown back, a white head and more black on the wings. These juveniles are gray-brown with dark legs while the juvenile of the lighter goose is grayish with a dark bill.

SIZE 28 inches (wingspan 58 inches)
DESCRIPTION Large waterbird with white plumage and black wing tips. Has a pinky-orange bill with a black "grin patch" and quite a long neck. Rusty markings on the neck in summer and a gray-blue tint to the wings that can be seen in flight
HABITAT Lakes, grasslands, and saltwater
SIMILAR SPECIES Similar to Ross's Goose but is larger with a longer neck and a flatter head with the distinctive "grin patch" on the bill

WOOD DUCK
(AIX SPONSA)

The *weep weep* cry of the Wood Duck can often be heard as it flies through the trees. It uses nesting boxes and is one of the few ducks to nest in trees about 50 feet from the ground using cavities which it lines with down. The female incubates 8–14 eggs for 28–32 days, with the young leaving the nest soon after hatching. They drop down from the trees after being called by their mother and follow her into the water but do not actually fly for about 7 weeks. The Wood Duck feeds on aquatic plants, fish, insects, fruit, and crustaceans and is found throughout the country at different times of the year although not usually in the breeding grounds during the winter.

SIZE 18½ inches

DESCRIPTION Female is gray-brown with white "spectacles" around the eye. Male has purple and glossy green head with a long crest, a black and white face, black back, buff flanks, and a chestnut breast

HABITAT Forest-edged lakes, swamps, ponds, and marshes

SIMILAR SPECIES Female is similar to female Mandarin Duck but with larger eye patch. Male Wood Duck has distinctive markings

MALLARD (ANAS PLATYRHYNCHOS)

SIZE 23 inches

DESCRIPTION Male has glossy green head and neck with a white ring around the base, a yellow bill, chestnut breast, and gray body. The female is mottled brown with an orange bill with black markings

HABITAT Shallow ponds and marshes

SIMILAR SPECIES Male has distinctive markings while the female is similar to other species but with black markings on the orange bill

The Mallard is a dabbling duck that nests near water, lining a hollow then laying 5–14 eggs. The female incubates them for 26–29 days and although the young soon leave the nest they do not fly for a further 8 weeks. It feeds on aquatic plants, insects, and small fish and can often be seen with just the ends of its tail sticking out of the water as it forages around in the shallows. The young are similar in color to the female but with olive-green bills. It is one of the most common ducks in America and the ancestor of most domestic ducks. It lives in the wild and is also at home in city parks if there is water present.

(ANAS ACUTA) NORTHERN PINTAIL

The Northern Pintail is found throughout most of America, breeding in the north then wintering in the south. It is a dabbling duck that likes to live in the open, feeding in the shallows searching for small fish, snails, and crustaceans. It nests in a hollow lined with plant material where the female incubates 6–12 eggs for about 26 days. The young leave the nest shortly after hatching but are not able to fly for a further 7 weeks. The juveniles are similar in color to the female. Between the breeding season and migration many of the males molt their feathers and develop an "eclipse" plumage making them resemble a browner and darker version of the female.

SIZE 20–26 inches

DESCRIPTION Male has a gray body with long black tail feathers. The head is brown with a white stripe and the breast is white. The female is a brownish color with a slightly shorter tail and grayish bill. Both have a metallic green-brown patch on the upper wing and a white band on the trailing edge

HABITAT Lakes, ponds, and marshes

SIMILAR SPECIES Markings on the male are distinctive. Female is similar to other species but larger

KING EIDER (SOMATERIA SPECTABILIS)

SIZE 22 inches

DESCRIPTION Male has an orange bill with an orange shield over it, white breast and wing patch, a black body, and white breast. Female is brown with darker crescent markings

HABITAT Coastal waters, tundra ponds, and the Great Lakes

SIMILAR SPECIES Female is similar to female Eider Duck but is smaller with crescent-shaped bars on body and has a more rounded head. Male is distinctive

The King Eider is a sea duck that is very common in the far north with many found on the Great Lakes. It breeds on tundra but winters at sea, frequently in openings in the pack ice. The migrations are spectacular with huge flocks, often consisting solely of females or males, traveling in long lines along the coast. It is capable of diving up to 180 feet to search for fish, crustaceans, mollusks, and starfish, achieving this by diving from the surface using its wings to propel itself through the water. The King Eider will nest in a down-filled hollow near water where 4–7 greeny-buff eggs are incubated by the female for about 23 days. The chicks leave soon after hatching.

(AYTHYA FULIGULA) TUFTED DUCK

The Tufted Duck is a diving duck and will search in the water for mollusks and aquatic plants, supplementing its diet with insects and frogs. The male is generally silent but gives a low whistle during courtship. The female makes a gruff growling call. It is an Old World species that often visits Alaska and in winter can be found along the east coast to Maryland and on the west coast to southern California. The Tufted Duck nests in vegetation near water where it lines a hollow with grass and down. The 6–10 greenish or buff-colored eggs are laid and then incubated by the female for 23–28 days. The down-covered chicks leave the nest soon after hatching. They eventually fly at about 7 weeks.

SIZE 17 inches

DESCRIPTION Female has gray-brown plumage, a white undertail and white at the base of the bill. The male has a black body with white sides. The round head is black with a long black tuft. Gray bill with a black tip

HABITAT Coastal lagoons, seashore, and sheltered ponds

SIMILAR SPECIES Similar to Ring-necked Duck but female lacks the pale cheeks and the male has white rather than gray sides and the long tuft on the head

CANVASBACK

(AYTHYA VALISINERIA)

The Canvasback is common throughout much of America, but is a very wary bird, tending to stay in the middle of lakes or bays. It only usually comes ashore to breed in the marshes in the northwest. Its population had decreased due to loss of habitat but now seems to have stabilized. It conceals its nest in tall vegetation near deep open water. The nest is woven into a tight cup from grass and lined with down. The female lays 7–9 greenish eggs which she incubates for 24–27 days. The chicks soon leave the nest and later fly at about 10–12 weeks. The Canvasback is a very deep diver and will often go down as much as 30 feet to find small invertebrates and the roots of aquatic plants.

SIZE 21 inches

DESCRIPTION Male has chestnut-colored head and neck with whitish sides and back, while female has pale brown head and neck with a brownish-gray body. Both have a distinctive "ski-slope" profile with a sloping forehead and long black bill

HABITAT Lakes, ponds, marshes, and bays

SIMILAR SPECIES Very similar to the Redhead and often found together but the forehead on the Canvasback slopes and the bill is black and longer. The Redhead has a contrasting stripe on the wing

COMMON GOLDENEYE
(BUCEPHALA CLANGULA)

SIZE 18½ inches

DESCRIPTION Females are mottled gray with a tawny head, a white ear spot, and white chest and belly. Males have a black head with a greenish gloss, a black back with white chest and sides, and a white spot on the head

HABITAT Rivers, lakes, open bays, and estuaries

SIMILAR SPECIES Similar to Barrow's Goldeneye which has a steeper forehead and a smaller bill. The male has a white crescent rather than a spot on the head and more black on the back

The nickname of this diving duck is Whistler due to the ringing sound its wings make in flight. It is found throughout most of America and lives in small flocks breeding around bogs or lakes near coniferous forests, then wintering in coastal areas or inland rivers and lakes. During the courtship display the male will snap his head backward and forward while the female lies in the water as if dead. It nests in trees laying 6–15 greenish eggs that are incubated for 27–32 days. The female, however, will not begin the incubation until the last one is laid. The young cannot fly until they are 8–9 weeks old, but drop from the nest a short time after hatching. The Common Goldeneye eats mollusks, crustaceans, and aquatic plants.

RUDDY DUCK
(OXYURA JAMAICENSIS)

In the courtship display the male erects his tail feathers so they nearly touch his head and flares the feathers over his eyes, then puffs up his neck and breast and drums the throat with his bill making the water bubble in front of him. The floating nest is anchored to vegetation and the 5–17 large eggs are incubated for 24 days. Both parents care for the young which fly at 6–7 weeks. It dives in deep water eating the seeds and foliage of aquatic plants, even the young ducklings dive when the young of other species would feed off the surface. The Ruddy Duck is common in many areas and is usually seen in large flocks breeding in freshwater wetlands then wintering on lakes or bays.

SIZE 15 inches

DESCRIPTION The female is a brownish color with pale cheeks that have a dark slash across them. The male is chestnut-brown with a dark cap, white cheeks and a bright blue bill in the breeding season. Tails are short and usually erect

HABITAT Lakes, ponds, rivers, and marshes

SIMILAR SPECIES The coloring and stiff feathers on the tail make this duck distinctive

COMMON MERGANSER (MERGUS MERGANSER)

SIZE 25 inches

DESCRIPTION Female has a gray body with a reddish head and a white throat. The male has a dark green head with a mainly white body, a black back, and a red bill

HABITAT Lakes, ponds, and rivers near woodlands

SIMILAR SPECIES Like the Mallard and Northern Shoveler it has a green head but the body coloring and shape are different. The female is similar to the Red-breasted Merganser but there is a sharper contrast between the neck and back coloring

The Common Merganser is often nicknamed Sawbill as it has a long, narrow bill with serrated edges and a hooked upper mandible which helps the duck catch and hold onto fish. It dives underwater to catch its prey, chasing small fish and frogs, newts, and aquatic invertebrates. It is usually seen in large flocks and is generally found on fresh water. Its nest is built in a tree cavity or among rocks and lined with down where 6–12 pale buff eggs are laid and incubated by the female. These hatch after a 28–32-day incubation with the chicks leaving the nest soon after but not flying until 9–10 weeks old. This species is common throughout most of North America at different times of the year.

(CORAGYPS ATRATUS) BLACK VULTURE

This New World Vulture is a carrion-feeder and often hunts in groups. It can spend hours searching for food using sight and scent and when a carcass is found the group feeds together. It can also be found in urban areas where it is quite useful in eliminating garbage and carrion. The 1–2 blotchy white eggs are laid in the shelter of a rock, a ledge, or on the ground. After 40 days' incubation the young will stay in the nest where they are cared for by both parents until they are 11 weeks old. The Black Vulture can be found all year round in the south but is rarely seen in the north. It has legal protection under the 1918 Migratory Bird Treaty Act.

SIZE 25 inches (wingspan 59 inches)
DESCRIPTION Black plumage with a white spot near the wing tips, a large gray head, and white feet. In flight the wings are broad and the short glides are punctuated with rapid flaps. The wings are held flat
HABITAT Urban areas and open countryside
SIMILAR SPECIES The Turkey Vulture which has a red head, longer tail, and black wings edged with gray. In flight it mainly glides with the wings held in a "V" shape

TURKEY VULTURE
(CATHARTES AURA)

The Turkey Vulture is a carrion-feeder that will spend most of its day searching for food using scent to source its prey. It is able to glide for hours by rocking slightly from side to side, barely using its wings. The female lays 1–3 white eggs blotched with red-brown on the bare ground, in a cave or in a hollow log. Both parents incubate them for 40 days and the young remain in the nest for a further 11 weeks. The juvenile has a darker head and bill and paler feet. The Turkey Vulture tends to roost in flocks, often with many birds feeding together from a carcass. It can be found all over North America and into southern Canada.

SIZE 27 inches (wingspan 67 inches)
DESCRIPTION Very large black bird with gray edges to the wings, yellow feet, long black tail, and a bare wrinkled red head. In flight the wings are held in the gliding position making a shallow "V" shape
HABITAT Open country, farms, woodlands, especially around dead trees
SIMILAR SPECIES Black Vulture which has a shorter tail, gray head, and white tips to the wings. In flight it will hold the wings flat when gliding, interspersed with rapid flaps

NORTHERN HARRIER (CIRCUS CYANEUS)

Size 18 inches (wingspan 44 inches)
Description Long wings and tail with a white rump. Male is gray above and white below with reddish spots. The female is dark brown above and lighter below with brown streaks
Habitat Prairies, open areas, marshes, and wetlands
Similar Species Shape and color make it distinctive

Previously known as the Marsh Hawk, this bird is a relentless hunter flying low over open areas. With the wings held in a slight "V" it pursues its prey often flying over 70 miles a day hunting for reptiles, frogs, rodents, and small birds. A nest is built on a platform of grass and reeds in marshes and 4–6 white eggs are laid. These are incubated by the female for about 32 days with the chicks leaving the nest after 5 weeks. The male provides the food but they are actually fed by the female. Juveniles are similar to females but a more cinnamon-brown below. The Northen Harrier is common throughout most of North America, spending summer in the north then migrating south for the winter.

(ACCIPITER STRIATUS) SHARP-SHINNED HAWK

The Sharp-shinned Hawk is the smallest of the North American accipiters – hawks that are adapted to their woodland habitat. It is found over much of North America at different times of the year. The female is larger than the male and is capable of flying faster, enabling it to catch larger or faster-flying prey. It hunts for small birds, rodents, or insects, flying at great speed through dense woodland. It builds its nest in a tree 10–60 feet from the ground, laying 4–5 bluish, spotted eggs which are incubated for 35 days by both parents. The young leave the nest after 2 months. The juvenile is brown above and white below with brown spotting.

SIZE 9–14 inches (wingspan 20–28 inches)

DESCRIPTION A hawk with short wings and a long, square, barred tail Plumage is blue-gray above and white below with rusty-colored barring. The female is similar in color but larger

HABITAT Mixed woods and forests.

SIMILAR SPECIES Similar plumage to Cooper's Hawk but this bird is smaller with a shorter, squarer tail

RED-TAILED HAWK
(BUTEO JAMAICENSIS)

The Red-tailed Hawk can often be observed sitting for long periods of time on posts or poles before gliding away to hunt for its prey that mainly consists of rodents. It kills them with its talons and if too large to swallow whole, will tear them with its sharp-hooked bill. This bird is generally found in open country where there are woods nearby for breeding. Its large nest is usually built 75 feet above the ground where 1–4 whitish eggs are incubated for 27–33 days. The chicks leave the nest after 5 weeks and juveniles have gray-brown tails with dark bars. It can be found over most of North America and well into Canada in the summer.

SIZE 22 inches (wingspan 50 inches)
DESCRIPTION Hawk with broad wings and a short tail. Plumage is dark on the back with pale mottling and white underneath with a dark belly band. Reddish tail which is white underneath and a heavy bill
HABITAT Open woodland, plains, and prairies
SIMILAR SPECIES Rough-legged Hawk which has a long white tail and Swainson's Hawk which lacks the mottling on the back and has a smaller bill

ROUGH-LEGGED HAWK (BUTEO LAGOPUS)

SIZE 22 inches (wingspan 56 inches)
DESCRIPTION Pale head, leg and chest with dark streaks. Back is brown with white underside and a dark belly band. Long white tail with dark tail bands. There is also a rarer darker version with darkish brown plumage with dark bands on a whitish undertail. The trailing edges of the wings are white tipped with black
HABITAT Marshes and open country
SIMILAR SPECIES The darker version is similar to the Ferruginous Hawk but with dark tail bands

The Rough-legged Hawk breeds in the tundra building its nest of twigs and moss on a cliff ledge. The 2–6 eggs are incubated for 29 days and the young leave after 6 weeks. The juvenile bird has a darker belly band and one dark-brown tail band. This bird spends the summer in the Arctic moving southward into central North America in the winter, settling on farmland and prairies. When in the Arctic it preys on ptarmigans and lemmings, feeding on rodents and small birds when it moves south. When hunting it will hover over one particular area while rapidly beating its wings. It is generally regarded as a "tame" species and will allow humans to approach at a fairly close range.

(BUTEO LINEATUS) RED-SHOULDERED HAWK

The Red-shouldered Hawk flies with many wingbeats followed by a glide but during the breeding season will soar in amazing displays while defending its territory. Being a forest bird, its nest is built high up in a tree near moving water. It then returns to the same nest each season, sprucing up the structure with fresh green material. The 2–5 whitish eggs are then incubated for 28 days by both parents with the chicks remaining in the nest for 5–6 weeks. It hunts for small birds and mammals, reptiles, frogs, and crayfish. This hawk is fairly common in Florida and California and in the southeast but is not as conspicuous as the Red-tailed Hawk, tending to perch below the treetops where it cannot therefore be seen so easily.

SIZE 17 inches (wingspan 40 inches)
DESCRIPTION Small woodland hawk with long tail and legs. The body and underwing are black with a rusty-colored shoulder patch. White bands on the wings and tail
HABITAT Forests and woodland near water
SIMILAR SPECIES Juvenile is similar to the juvenile Broad-winged Hawk but larger

OSPREY
(PANDION HALIAETUS)

The Osprey feeds on fish which it catches in its talons by plunging into water feet first. Its nest is constructed from sticks in a tall tree or rock pinnacle sited near water and the birds will return to the same one each year, adding to the structure each season. Two to four buff-colored eggs blotched with brown are incubated by the female for 1 month. The white-colored chicks then leave the nest after about 2 months. In flight this bird has long, narrow wings that are slightly arched with a bend at the wrist. The juveniles are very similar in appearance to the adult with additional white scaling on the back. This bird's population was once threatened by the use of DDT but since its ban the bird's numbers have increased considerably.

SIZE Up to 23 inches (wingspan 63 inches)
DESCRIPTION Dark brown plumage on the upper body with white below. White head has dark eye streak and a slight crest. Has long narrow wings that are held in a slightly arched position in flight
HABITAT Mainly coastal areas and some inland lakes and rivers
SIMILAR SPECIES Sometimes confused with gulls in flight but has a distinct color and shape

GOLDEN EAGLE
(AQUILA CHRYSAETOS)

The Golden Eagle is an amazing flier and hunter, soaring with its large wings held flat. It travels fast enough to take ptarmigans and grouse in the air and preys on rabbits, prairie dogs, and squirrels on the ground. It is able to attack mammals up to the size of a deer. The eyrie is made of masses of sticks and built in a tall tree or on a cliff and the male will often defend breeding territories of up to 75 square miles. Two whitish, brown-blotched eggs are incubated by both birds for 44 days and the chicks leave after 10 weeks. It is a very solitary bird that is occasionally seen in pairs but rarely in groups, preferring isolated areas away from humans.

SIZE 30 inches (wingspan 80 inches)
DESCRIPTION Very large bird of prey with dark brown plumage, a golden nape, and feathered legs. There are faint bands on the tail
HABITAT Mountains and forests, remote open areas
SIMILAR SPECIES Adult is quite distinctive but the juvenile is similar to the juvenile Bald Eagle but with a smaller head, a longer tail and white markings on the tail and under wings

BALD EAGLE
(HALIAEETUS LEUCOCEPHALUS)

The Bald Eagle is a very skilled hunter and feeds predominantly on fish. It is also renowned for stealing fish from Ospreys and may congregate near spawning runs which are easy targets. This eagle was endangered in the 1970s but the banning of pesticides and introduction of conservation programs have increased its population. It has been the national symbol of America since 1782. It builds its eyrie from sticks in a tree up to 150 feet from the ground and near water. It returns to the same one each year, adding to the structure and weight: some nests have been known to weigh up to 1000 lb. Both parents will incubate 1–3 dull, whitish-colored eggs for up to 35 days with the young birds leaving after 10 weeks.

SIZE 31 inches (wingspan 80 inches)
DESCRIPTION A large bird of prey with a brown-black body and yellow bill. The head, neck, and tail are white
HABITAT Open areas or forests near to water
SIMILAR SPECIES Adult bird is distinctive but the juvenile is similar to the juvenile Golden Eagle but with a larger head, a shorter tail, and blotchy, less precise markings on the tail and underwings

CRESTED CARACARA (CARACARA PLANCUS)

SIZE 23 inches (wingspan 50 inches)
DESCRIPTION A falcon with a long neck and long legs. Plumage is black-brown with a whitish chest and throat. Red facial skin and a black-brown crest. Barred underparts
HABITAT Desert and open savannah
SIMILAR SPECIES Color and shape make it distinctive

The Crested Caracara is a tropical bird that is found only as far north as Texas, parts of Florida and occasionally southern Arizona and Louisiana. It soars with the wings held flat as it hunts for small animals and insects although it mainly feeds on carrion and is often seen on the ground with vultures. It spends quite a large amount of time on the ground using its long legs to aid hunting. The nest is built high in the trees where 2–4 eggs are incubated for 28 days with the young taking up to 12 months to fly independently. It is often referred to as the "Mexican Eagle" and appears on the flag of Mexico.

(FALCO SPARVERIUS) AMERICAN KESTREL

This bird is a familiar sight sitting on a high perch or hovering in the air as it searches for prey. Then it plunges to the ground in the hunt for mice, insects, or frogs. Its voice is a very excited *killy, killy, killy*. This is the smallest and most common of American falcons and is found across the country although those living in the far north will migrate south for the winter. It was formerly known as the Sparrow Hawk. It does not build a nest, but uses a hollow tree or an old magpie nest instead. After 3–6 eggs are laid they are incubated mainly by the female for around 30 days with the young able to leave the nest after a further month.

SIZE 10½ inches (wingspan 23 inches)
DESCRIPTION Small bird with a long tail. Russet crown, back, and tail with two black stripes on a white face. Hooked bill. Male has blue-gray on its wings and head, a buff breast and nape, and white underparts with dark spots
HABITAT Open wooded areas, deserts, farmlands, prairies, cities, and suburbs
SIMILAR SPECIES Male is similar to the male Merlin but with a russet tail and back

MERLIN (FALCO COLUMBARIUS)

SIZE 12 inches (wingspan 25 inches)

DESCRIPTION Male has blue-gray upper parts, buff underparts with light brown streaks and a black tail band. The juveniles and females are brown above with buff tail bands

HABITAT Towns, wooded prairies, and open woods

SIMILAR SPECIES Male resembles the American Kestrel but with broader wings and no russet markings on the back or tail. The Prairie and Peregrine Falcons lack the tail bands and are much larger

The Merlin flies at low levels with rapid, shallow wingbeats. It preys on small birds, mice, lizards, and large insects and will fly above the target, suddenly dropping to catch the victim in its talons. The bird then takes its prey to a perch where it is plucked before being presented to its mate who will then take it back to the nest. Three to six eggs are laid in tree holes, abandoned nests or on the ground. After 30 days' incubation the young remain in the nest for a further month. The Merlin can be found in open country across North America, spending the summer in the north before migrating south for the winter. Those in the central areas will stay all year round.

(FALCO MEXICANUS) PRAIRIE FALCON

The Prairie Falcon hunts for squirrels, birds, and rodents. It spends time searching for prey from perches high above the ground then with rapid wingbeats interspersed with short glides it swoops down on its prey from behind. The victim is caught in the falcon's talons as it swoops to the ground. The larger female rarely builds a nest, laying the 3–6 reddish, dark-spotted eggs on a ledge or in an abandoned nest. The young are incubated for a month and then leave the nest after about 6 weeks. The juveniles are darker than the adults with less contrast and heavier streaks on the undersides. It is quite a common bird that is found in the west of the country throughout the year.

SIZE 17½ inches (wingspan 40 inches)

DESCRIPTION Large falcon with a long tail and pointed wings. Light brown plumage above with pale barring and white below with dark streaks. Black patch at the base of the wings that can be seen in flight

HABITAT Prairies, deserts, open areas in mountains, and dry grassland

SIMILAR SPECIES Resembles Peregrine Falcon but lacks the black crown. Similar to juvenile and female Merlin but is larger and minus the tail bands

PEREGRINE FALCON
(FALCO PEREGRINUS)

The Peregrine Falcon is an extremely fast flier and will make amazing dives to catch small birds in mid-air with one bird recording a speed of 275 miles an hour. It will also feed on small mammals and large insects. Like many other falcons it does not build a nest so the 2–4 reddish, darker flecked eggs are laid on building ledges, cliffs, or rocky outcrops and then incubated by both parents for 4 weeks with the chicks leaving after a further 5–6 weeks. This falcon was once common across North America but the use of DDT and other pesticides nearly led to its extinction in the east. Now that these chemicals have been banned, captive-breeding programs have led to the reintroduction of the Peregrine Falcon in some areas.

Size 17 inches (wingspan 41 inches)
Description A large falcon with blue-gray plumage above, a black head, and a finely barred whitish breast. The female is browner in color
Habitat Cliffs, cities, and open wetlands
Similar Species The Merlin and Prairie Falcon are similar but lack the black head

GRAY PARTRIDGE (PERDIX PERDIX)

SIZE 12½ inches
DESCRIPTION Brown-gray coloring and red barring on the flanks. Orange-red face and throat. Male has a chestnut patch on his belly
HABITAT Grassy fields and open farmland
SIMILAR SPECIES Similar to the Chukar but with different coloring

The Gray Partridge is a ground-dwelling bird that will search for grain and other seeds on the ground. It rarely flies very far even when flushed out. The nest is built by lining a shallow depression in the ground with leaves and grass. It is hidden in the surrounding vegetation and there the female will lay up to 16 olive-colored eggs. After 26 days' incubation the young leave the nest immediately after hatching but it is a further 2–3 weeks before they are capable of flying and then they stay with the female until the following spring. The Gray Partridge is an Old World species brought into North America in the 19th century and released as a game bird. Since then it has spread across Central America.

(DENDRAGAPUS OBSCURUS) BLUE GROUSE

The Blue Grouse is a ground-dweller that feeds on pine needles in the winter and eats berries, seeds, and insects in the summer. This bird tends to be seen on its own and prefers to inhabit areas near large clearings. The male displays in the spring by standing high in the trees spreading out his tail and inflating the neck sac. He will also fly down and strut around with the tail still spread and the wings dragging on the ground, hooting to attract females. A scrape is lined with pine needles and grass and hidden under the shelter of a rock or log. The female incubates 6–10 eggs for 26 days with the chicks staying in the nest for about 12 weeks.

SIZE 20 inches

DESCRIPTION Large bird with a short bill and a long tail. The male has a yellow-orange comb over each eye and blue-gray plumage. The tail is dark with a gray tip. It has a purplish or yellow neck sac that is inflated when displaying, surrounded by white feathers. The female has mottled gray-brown plumage

HABITAT Mountain slopes, open coniferous or mixed woodland, and brushy lowland

SIMILAR SPECIES Female resembles female Spruce Grouse but is bigger with a longer tail. She lacks the barring on the underparts

SAGE GROUSE
(CENTROCERCUS UROPHASIANUS)

The Sage Grouse is a ground-dwelling bird that feeds mainly on sagebrush buds and leaves. In spring groups of males join together on the traditional display ground known as a lek. They attract females by performing a dance strutting and bobbing about. During this process they fan their tails and inflate their chests to reveal 2 yellow-green air sacs that they are able to inflate and deflate rapidly to make a loud popping noise. A male will often mate with several females. The female uses a depression in the ground under a sagebush in which to lay 7–12 greenish and spotted eggs that are incubated for 26 days. The young remain with the mother for some time. The population of Sage Grouses is now decreasing due to the disappearance of its preferred habitat.

SIZE 28 inches
DESCRIPTION Gray-streaked plumage above with black below. Long pointed tail. Male has a black throat and white breast
HABITAT Plains and sagebrush foothills
SIMILAR SPECIES Resembles Sharp-tailed Grouse but is larger with a black belly

ROCK PTARMIGAN
(LAGOPUS MUTUS)

SIZE 14 inches

DESCRIPTION In winter both adults have white plumage with a black tail and bill and a black eye line. The feet are feathered. In summer the male has dark brown plumage with white wings, and a white belly. The female in summer has mottled brown plumage and white wings

HABITAT Tundra and high rocky slopes

SIMILAR SPECIES The male with his winter plumage resembles the Willow Ptarmigan but has the distinctive black eye line. It is also similar to the White-tailed Ptarmigan but has a black tail. In summer the male is again similar to the Willow but less red in color. The female Willow and Rock Ptarmigan, are very similar

This ptarmigan feeds on seeds, fruits, buds, and insects in the summer but in winter is confined to buds and twigs. Its stomach is adapted to this diet having special bacteria enabling it to digest woody material. Another adaption is the feathered feet which act as snowshoes, allowing the bird to walk on soft snow. The feathers are hollow and filled with air which provide the bird with some insulation. Sheltered scrapes in the tundra are where the female lays her 6–9 buff-colored eggs, but as many as 16 can be produced. The male defends the territory while the female incubates the eggs for around 21 days. The chicks are very quick to leave the nest and fly within 10 days.

RING-NECKED PHEASANT
(PHASIANUS COLCHICUS)

This bird is renowned for being a fast runner and for the noise it makes when flushed out of the undergrowth as it rises rapidly and vertically into the air. It feeds on nuts, seeds, and berries, establishing itself in open countryside and particularly in farmland where food is plentiful. The male will mate with a number of females who lay their eggs in a scrape lined with grass hidden amongst grass or weeds. The 7–14 buff or pale olive eggs are then incubated for 24 days with the young chicks flying after about 2 weeks. A native of Asia, the Ring-necked Pheasant was introduced into North America in the 19th century and is now common in many areas.

SIZE 21 inches (female), 33 inches (male)

DESCRIPTION The male is bronze with green, black, and brown mottling. Its head is a glossy green-black with red eye patches, and a white collar. It has a long, pointed, bronze tail barred with black and short rounded wings. The female has buff-colored plumage with a shorter, barred tail

HABITAT Prairies, brushy areas, fertile croplands, and open country

SIMILAR SPECIES Male is very distinctive. Female is similar to female Sharp-tailed Grouse but is a larger bird with a longer tail and the barring underneath is absent

WILD TURKEY

(MELEAGRIS GALLOPAVO)

The Wild Turkey feeds on the ground searching for berries, seeds, insects, and nuts and then roosts in the trees at night. Populations have dwindled in recent years due to hunting and loss of habitat but numbers are now on the increase with reintroduction and careful management. In the breeding period the Wild Turkey will display by spreading his tail, swelling out the wattles, and rattling his wings while calling out a gobbling, mating cry. This will be responded to by at least 10 females who eventually each lay 8–16 buff, spotted eggs in shallow, lined depressions in the woods. After a month's incubation the chicks leave very quickly and fly within a few weeks. They remain, however, with the mother until the following spring.

SIZE 37 inches (female), 46 inches (male)

DESCRIPTION A very large bird with a long tail with black bands near the tip. Male is glossy brown with a bare, pale bluish head, and red wattles. A long, dark breast tuft. The female is smaller and duller and sometimes lacks the breast tuft

HABITAT Oak and mesquite brush, and deciduous woodlands

SIMILAR SPECIES The size and shape make this bird distinctive

NORTHERN BOBWHITE
(COLINUS VIRGINIANUS)

SIZE 9¾ inches

DESCRIPTION Plumage is mottled red-brown with striped flanks and a short, gray tail. The female has a buff throat and eye stripe while the male has a white throat and eye stripe with a black area between the two that extends under the throat

HABITAT Open pine woods, farms, and brushy areas

SIMILAR SPECIES Size and color make it distinctive within its range

The Northern Bobwhite is usually the only quail to be found in the southeast. It is a ground-dweller that feeds on berries, leaves, seeds, and nuts. It typically lives in flocks or coveys of around 25–30 birds, except in the summer, and these will often roost together in a ring with their heads facing outward so they can each escape from danger easily. A shallow depression lined with grass and hidden amongst plants or brush is where the female lays 10–15 creamy-colored eggs. Both parents incubate the eggs. After hatching, the chicks are fed for a week and then have to find their own food, but they remain with their parents until the following spring. Juveniles are smaller and duller than the adults.

CALIFORNIA QUAIL
(CALLIPEPLA CALIFORNICA)

The California Quail lives in large coveys during the fall and winter and can often be seen in yards, gardens, and city parks. This bird is a ground-dweller that is easily frightened and hence "sentries" will be posted when the coveys are feeding. It lives on nuts, berries, seeds, and insects. At night it roosts in the trees for safety and when on the ground it is more likely to run than fly if startled. In the spring the coveys break into breeding pairs and the female lays 12–15 eggs in a scrape lined with grass that is hidden under a bush or rock. The female incubates the eggs for 3 weeks and the young fly after a further 10 days.

SIZE 10 inches

DESCRIPTION A small bird with a brown back and blue-gray breast. Sides are streaked with white and there is a scaly pattern on the belly. Forward-curving plume on the head. Longish tail. Male has brown crown and black throat edged with white. The female has a smaller plume

HABITAT Meadows, suburbs, brushy areas, and open woodland

SIMILAR SPECIES Very similar to Gambel's Quail but lacks the chestnut-colored flanks and has scaling

AMERICAN COOT
(FULICA AMERICANA)

This bird feeds in a similar way to a duck diving to the bottom hunting for fish and mollusks but it will also dabble on the surface to find insects and pond weed or forage on lawns in urban areas. To fly from the surface of the water it needs to patter along the surface into the wind until it can lift off. If startled, however, it tends to dash to the safety of the shore or the reeds. Platforms of marsh vegetation and reeds are built on the edges of open water where 8–20 eggs are laid then incubated for 25 days. The chicks are independent within 7–8 weeks. The American Coot is a widespread species that lives in large flocks, often becoming quite tame in urban areas.

SIZE 15½ inches

DESCRIPTION Marshbird with a black head and neck and a whitish forehead shield with a reddish color on the upper edge. The bill is whitish with a dark band near to the tip. Black plumage and large lobed feet

HABITAT Lakes, ponds, marshes, and slow-moving rivers

SIMILAR SPECIES Resembles the Common Moorhen which has a white line on the plumage and a red facial shield

PURPLE GALLINULE
(PORPHYRULA MARTINICA)

This marshbird is able to fly but is rather reluctant to do so and rarely swims. It feeds on grain, seeds, insects, frogs, birds' eggs, and vegetation. The nest is shaped like a shallow cup and made from reeds and grass stems. Here 5–10 buff eggs spotted with brown are laid, with both parents incubating them. One bird will bring its incubating partner a leaf which will be added to the nest before they swap over in a "changing of the guard" type ceremony. Both parents feed their young and the chicks leave soon after hatching. Warm-water marshes are the Purple Gallinule's preferred habitat and it is generally found in the south and around the Gulf, but winters are spent in southern Florida and Argentina.

SIZE 13 inches
DESCRIPTION Marshbird with a bright purple-blue head, neck, and underparts and a pale blue forehead shield. The bill is red and yellow and the back a brown-green. It has long yellow legs and large yellow feet that allow it to walk across marsh vegetation
HABITAT Marshes, lagoons, and freshwater swamps
SIMILAR SPECIES The coloring makes this bird distinctive

COMMON MOORHEN (GALLINULA CHLOROPUS)

SIZE 14 inches

DESCRIPTION A marshbird with black-gray plumage on the head and neck. The back is a brownish-olive color and the underparts are slate with a white streak visible on the flanks. A red bill with a yellow tip and long yellow legs and large yellow feet

HABITAT Weedy edges of rivers, lakes, ponds, and marshes

SIMILAR SPECIES Resembles Purple Gallinule and American Coot but can be distinguished by the white streak and the red facial shield

Once known as the Common Gallinule, the Common Moorhen is seen frequently throughout much of the country. This bird uses its long legs and large feet to wade across the floating vegetation. It eats a varied diet including tadpoles, spiders, insect larvae, fruit, and seeds. Grass stems and reeds are used to build the nest which is sited in marsh vegetation about 12 inches above the water level, often with a ramp to lead it down to the water. There 8–12 eggs are laid that are incubated for 3 weeks by both parents. The young chicks will then leave the nest soon after hatching. The juvenile is duller in color with a dark bill and lacks the red facial shield.

(CHARADRIUS VOCIFERUS) KILLDEER

This bird nests in depressions on the ground where 4 eggs are laid and then incubated by both parents for 26 days. Chicks soon leave the nest and are able to fly within the month. Adults will fiercely defend the nest, and if any animal approaches may well spread their wings, scold the animal and even fly at it. Should a predator approach the nest, the adult Killdeer will play wounded as if it has a broken wing gradually luring it away to keep the young safe. The Killdeer's name echoes its *kill-deeah* call. It is a very common bird that is found in the south throughout the year, spreading further north in the summer. It feeds in loose flocks on insects, snails, and earthworms.

SIZE 10½ inches

DESCRIPTION Gray-brown back with white underparts. Two black bars across the upper chest. Long, pale gray legs and feet and a long, thin, dark bill. Long tail and slender wings. In flight the reddish rump and a white wing stripe are visible

HABITAT Meadows, prairies, lakes, and river shores

SIMILAR SPECIES The two black bars across the chest make this bird distinctive

SANDHILL CRANE
(GRUS CANADENSIS)

Like all other cranes the Sandhill Crane is an amazing dancer. It is capable of skipping and hopping, leaping as much as 20 feet into the air. It is usually seen in flocks of 20–100 individuals and feeds on insects, small animals, and spilled grain. It breeds on the Arctic tundra and also in isolated marshes further south where a large pile of vegetation is used to make a nest for 2 eggs. After both parents have incubated these for about a month the young quickly leave the nest. They are capable of flight at 10 months but stay with the parents until the following spring. The Sandhill Crane is quite a common bird spending the winter in the far south and the summer in the north.

SIZE 34–42 inches (wingspan 73–90 inches)
DESCRIPTION A tall, long-legged bird with gray plumage that sometimes has rusty stains caused by ferrous mud that transfers from the bill when preening. The rump has a bushy tuft of feathers. Reddish cap on the head with a long neck that is outstretched in flight
HABITAT Tundra, marshes, grasslands, and grainfields
SIMILAR SPECIES Resembles Great Blue Heron which has a longer bill and lacks the clump of feathers on the rump. The heron flies with the neck folded back

AMERICAN OYSTERCATCHER
(HAEMATOPUS PALLIATUS)

SIZE 18½ inches

DESCRIPTION A coastal bird with broad wings and a short tail. Plumage is dark brown on the back with white underparts and white wing and tail patches. Black head and long orange-red bill

HABITAT Coastal areas and mudflats

SIMILAR SPECIES The plumage and bill make it distinctive

This oystercatcher can be found along the southern Pacific coast and along most of the Atlantic and is still expanding northward. It feeds on oysters, limpets, starfish, crabs, and worms using the impressive bill to dislodge animals from rocks and prise open shells. It feeds in small flocks in the winter but is found in pairs or family groups in the spring and summer. The female uses hollows in the sand in which to lay 2–4 greenish-buff spotted eggs that are incubated by the parents for 23–28 days. The young, downy chicks which leave the nest soon after hatching are independent within 5 weeks. Juveniles are similar to adults but with a dark tip to the bill and light scaling on the back.

AMERICAN AVOCET
(RECURVIROSTRA AMERICANA)

The Avocet is a common sight in the west in the summer and along the southern coastline in the winter. It uses its long bill by sweeping it from side to side through the water and mud, finding aquatic insects and shrimp-type crustaceans by touch. It will also take insects from the surface of the water or when flying in mid-air. Small groups nest on open mudflats or muddy patches in the grass but each pair has its own space. Four blotched olive eggs are laid in a depression lined with grass and if any predator approaches, the bird screams to alert all the surrounding birds to mob the attacker. After 21–28 days' incubation the chicks are then independent after 5 weeks.

SIZE 18 inches
DESCRIPTION A wading bird with very long, thin, gray legs. Plumage is black and white on the back with white underparts. The neck and head are cinnamon in summer and gray in winter. The long, thin bill is upturned at the end (more so in the female)
HABITAT Marshes, mudflats, shallow lakes, beaches, and ponds
SIMILAR SPECIES Very distinctive

GREATER YELLOWLEGS (TRINGA MELANOLEUCA)

SIZE 14 inches

DESCRIPTION Gray-brown plumage with black and white mottling on the back with white below. Rump is white and tail is barred. Long bright yellow legs and a long bill that is slightly upturned. In its breeding plumage the breast and throat are heavily streaked, the flanks are barred with black and the back is more darkly marked

HABITAT Marshes, bogs, ponds, streams, and swamps

SIMILAR SPECIES Very similar to the Lesser Yellowlegs but larger. This, however, is only noticeable if the two stand together

Once known as Tattler or Tell-tale, this noisy sandpiper cries to signal the approach of an intruder using a loud, whistled call of 3–5 notes. A common bird, the Greater Yellowlegs winters in the south and spends summers in the north. It uses the northern swamps, the taiga and damp, boreal forests to breed, laying 4 eggs in a shallow scrape in woodland. After about 21 days' incubation the young are then independent within 20 days. During the winter it can be seen feeding in flocks with other wading birds, but normally wades into deeper water than most birds. Using its long bill it sweeps the water to catch invertebrates or to stab at small fish, supplementing these with water snails and aquatic insects.

(CATOPTROPHORUS SEMIPALMATUS) WILLET

The Willet is a noisy bird that will often echo its name calling *pill-o-will-o-willet*. It feeds in small but widely spaced flocks searching for small marine animals, seeds, and insects. It winters in the south along both North American coasts but is restricted to the Atlantic and Gulf coasts in the summer, along with some areas in the west. A clutch of 3–4 eggs is laid in a cup made from grass or in a scrape in the ground. Incubation then takes 21–30 days with the female caring for the chicks until they are independent. Although a shore bird, it will often perch in trees or on fences and when landing holds its wings above its head as if about to fly.

SIZE 15 inches

DESCRIPTION A wading bird with sand-gray plumage on the back and white below. Long, thick, gray legs and a long, gray bill. In the breeding season plumage is heavily mottled. In flight the wings have a black patch and trailing edge with a broad, white band in between

HABITAT Moist prairies, wetlands, salt marshes, and coastal beaches

SIMILAR SPECIES Stockier and larger than other sandpipers

LEAST SANDPIPER (CALIDRIS MINUTILLA)

SIZE 6 inches

DESCRIPTION Small bird with yellow legs and a short, thin, black bill slightly curved down at the tip. In winter the plumage is gray above and white below. In its breeding plumage the back is brown-gray while the head and upper breast are sometimes tinged with rust. White belly

HABITAT Tundra, northern wetlands, marshes, ponds, and rivers

SIMILAR SPECIES Very similar to Western and Semipalmated Sandpipers but has yellow legs with darker plumage on the back

This is one of the smallest of the North American sandpipers and is sometimes known as a mud peep due to its liking for oozy tidal flats. In spring and fall it can be seen inland as it migrates from the breeding grounds in the north to spend winter in the south or South America. As with other sandpipers the male performs a courtship flight by rising with his wings bent down and vibrating while he flutters in circles, trilling repeatedly with a varied song. This bird breeds in the Arctic tundra where 4 eggs are laid in a depression then incubated for 21 days with the chicks soon leaving the nest. It feeds on aquatic insects and marine animals.

(CALIDRIS ALPINA) DUNLIN

This bird is sometimes referred to as the Red-backed Sandpiper due to the color of its breeding plumage. Large flocks can be seen on both coasts from fall until spring, and summers are spent on the Arctic tundra where breeding takes place. Four buff, greenish brown spotted eggs are laid in a grass-lined scrape with both parents incubating them for 3 weeks. Both then care for the chicks which leave the nest soon after hatching. Juveniles are brown with buff undersides and dark streaks on the breast and flanks. The Dunlin feeds on wet surfaces, tapping with the bill slightly open to search for mollusks, aquatic insects, and small crustaceans. If disturbed these birds rise into the air in a swirling mass.

SIZE 8½ inches

DESCRIPTION A small shorebird with a long bill that curves down slightly. In the breeding season the adult plumage is gray-brown on the neck, head, and upper breast, the back is reddish-brown while the belly and flanks are whitish with a black patch on the belly. In winter the plumage is gray-brown above and whitish below

HABITAT Marshes, tundra, ponds, and mudflats

SIMILAR SPECIES Very similar to the Rock Sandpiper which has a dark gray lower breast patch and lighter colored legs

COMMON SNIPE
(GALLINAGO GALLINAGO)

Previously known as Wilson's Snipe, this bird is found across most of North America excluding the Rockies. It is very solitary and hence is only usually seen in flight. The Common Snipe feeds on invertebrates and worms using its flexible bill to dig deep into the ground. During a fascinating courtship display it will produce great climbs prior to diving with the outer tail feathers spread that produce a bleating sound. The breeding season is spent in the northern half of the continent and the nest is built in hidden depressions in the ground. The female incubates 4 olive-brown eggs for up to 3 weeks, both parents feed the chicks and the young are then independent within 20 days. After the young are reared the Common Snipe moves south for the winter.

SIZE 10½ inches
DESCRIPTION Adult has light and dark stripes along the head and brown mottled plumage on its back that is streaked with white. Dark barring to flanks. Long pointed bill and short legs and wings. Flight is fast, creating a zig-zag pattern
HABITAT Damp inland areas such as marshes, ponds, and fields
SIMILAR SPECIES Shape and bill make this species distinctive

PARASITIC JAEGER
(STERCORARIUS PARASITICUS)

SIZE 19 inches

DESCRIPTION A bulky-looking bird with a short, pointed tail and long pointed wings. In flight wings show a white patch underneath and a white flash at the tip. Two color variations exist: the darker version is a uniform dark brown, and the light version has a brown back and is white below with a white neck and a yellow tint to the cheek, black cap, and a brown-gray wash across the chest

HABITAT Open lakes, offshore, and the Great Lakes

SIMILAR SPECIES Light version is similar to the Long-tailed Jaeger but has the brown-gray wash on the chest and the white wing markings but lacks the long tail streamers

The Parasitic Jaeger is normally seen off the southeast and southwest coasts but is rarely seen inland. The name jaeger comes from the translation of the German word for hunter – on its breeding ground it will fly low over the tundra to snatch eggs and prey on lemmings and young birds, while in the winter it steals from other seabirds, forcing them to drop their catch. It breeds on the Arctic tundra where 2 olive, brown-spotted eggs are laid in a depression in the ground, sometimes lined with lichens. Both parents incubate the clutch for up to 4 weeks, with the chicks leaving the nest after a further 5 weeks. The juvenile plumage is a uniform dark color.

GREAT BLACK-BACKED GULL
(LARUS MARINUS)

The Great Black-backed Gull is the largest gull in the world and is a scavenger and a predator. Whenever it mixes with other gulls this bird will generally dominate them, often stealing their food. It feeds on fish, the eggs and young of other seabirds, and is also happy to scavenge in garbage dumps and eat carrion. Nests are built in colonies using moss, seaweed, and grass where 2–3 eggs are incubated for about a month. The young, which soon leave the nest, eventually fly after 8 weeks. The plumage takes 4 years to mature with noticeable changes taking place each year. This gull is very common along the northeast coast and can also be found slightly inland. It is still expanding its range to the south.

SIZE 30 inches

DESCRIPTION Black upperparts with white undersides and pink legs. Head is white with pale eyes and a yellow bill with reddish spot near the tip. In flight, wings are black on top with a white trailing edge and white below with a white rump

HABITAT Coasts, shores of large rivers and lakes, and the Great Lakes

SIMILAR SPECIES Distinctive due to its size. First-winter bird resembles first-winter Herring Gull but head and underparts are lighter in color

HERRING GULL (LARUS ARGENTATUS)

SIZE 25 inches

DESCRIPTION A gray back and white underparts with pink legs and feet. Head and neck are white with a heavy yellow bill with a red spot. The pale eyes are surrounded by a red orbital ring. In winter the wings become gray with a narrow strip of white along the trailing edge and white spots on the black wing tips. The neck is streaked with brown and the red spot on the bill becomes dusky-colored

HABITAT Lakes, rivers, coasts, landfills, and fishing docks

SIMILAR SPECIES Often mistaken for several other large gulls as the plumage and size varies depending on the age of the bird

The Herring Gull is a scavenger that helpfully cleans up beaches and harbors. However, it also preys on the eggs and young of other birds, fish, and small crustaceans. As it is happy to eat virtually anything available the population is continuing to expand and is beginning to drive out weaker species. Breeding takes place in large colonies on cliffs or islets with seaweed and grass used to build nests on the ground where 2–3 eggs are laid. The chicks peck at the red spot on the parent's bill when they want to be fed with the regurgitated food that the adult provides. It takes 4 years for the plumage to mature, with each phase being quite different which makes this a hard bird to identify.

(LARUS DELAWARENSIS) RING-BILLED GULL

The Ring-billed Gull feeds on worms, mollusks, insects, and grasshoppers but is also very happy to scavenge from garbage dumps and seaside developments where there are plenty of food sources and people willing to feed them. It is a very widespread bird and the population is continuing to expand due to the availability of food. Breeding takes place in colonies, often alongside the California Gull and nests are built on the ground from grass and stems. Three eggs are laid and both parents incubate the eggs which take about 25 days to hatch. Both birds feed the young chicks with regurgitated food and they soon leave the nest taking about a month to fledge and 3 years to reach mature plumage.

SIZE 17½ inches

DESCRIPTION Pale gray back and white underparts with yellow legs and feet. The head and neck are white with a yellow bill ringed with black near the tip. Pale eyes are surrounded by a red orbital ring. In winter the nape has a brown wash and the wings become gray above with white on the trailing edge and underneath while the black wing tips have a small white spot

HABITAT Lakes, rivers, and beaches

SIMILAR SPECIES Similar to the Mew Gull which lacks the black ring on the bill. The Herring Gull has more pink-colored legs and heavier streaking on the neck. The California Gull has red and black on the bill with darker eyes. More black can be seen on the wing tips when the California is in flight

COMMON TERN (STERNA HIRUNDO)

SIZE 14½ inches

DESCRIPTION In the breeding season it has gray upperparts and a pale breast and belly, a red bill with a black tip and a black cap on the head. In the winter the forehead becomes white with a dark patch on the back of the neck and the crown and a dark bar on the shoulder. In flight the gray wings have a darker gray wedge near the tip of the upper wing

HABITAT Marshes, lakes, and coasts

SIMILAR SPECIES Very similar to the Arctic and Forster's Tern but the Arctic has a red bill, a longer tail and shorter legs, while Forster's has a more orange-colored bill and silver primaries

The Common Tern flies slowly over water, often hovering to locate its prey before diving to catch predominantly fish and but also aquatic invertebrates. It nests in colonies on beaches or islands using a scrape in the ground to lay 2–3 eggs and will fiercely defend its territory, even striking at humans who threaten it. Both parents then incubate the eggs for about 24 days and the young chicks are able to fly after 4 weeks. This bird takes 3 years to reach mature plumage. It is widespread and abundant, breeding in Canada and northern America then wintering in the Southern Hemisphere. It was hunted for its feathers in the 1800s and almost reached extinction but populations recovered in the following century.

(CHLIDONIAS NIGER) BLACK TERN

The Black Tern breeds in small, dense colonies on lakeshores or freshwater marshes. The floating nest is made from marsh vegetation where 2–3 buff eggs blotched with brown are incubated by both parents for about 3 weeks. Once the young have hatched they will remain in the nest for 2–3 weeks before they begin to fly. It feeds on crustaceans, insects, and small fish, hovering over the water before dipping to catch its prey near the surface of the water or catching insects on the wing. Mainly an inland bird, it can only be seen in the summer, after which it migrates to the Southern Hemisphere. The population of this tern is on the decline due to loss of habitat.

SIZE 9¾ inches

DESCRIPTION Small bird with a short tail that is slightly forked. Short black bill and dark legs. Dark gray plumage above with a dark crown, ear patch and shoulder bar and white underparts. In the breeding season it is mainly black with a dark gray tail, wings and back and white undertail coverts. The dark gray upper wing and light gray underwing can be seen in flight

HABITAT Lakes, ponds, and freshwater marshes

SIMILAR SPECIES Plumage and size make it distinctive

BLACK SKIMMER
(RYNCHOPS NIGER)

Once known as the Cutwater, the Black Skimmer feeds by flying just above the surface of the water, usually at night, with the tip of the lower bill in the water. In this way it is able to scoop up small fish and crustaceans. The lower bill is up to an inch longer than the upper and grows more quickly due to the continual wearing by the water. It nests in colonies on sandy beaches where up to 5 eggs are laid in a scrape in the sand. After hatching the young will stay close to the nest. It is a coastal bird that can be found round the Southern Atlantic and Pacific but moves as far north as New Hampshire in the summer.

SIZE 18 inches

DESCRIPTION Black upperparts with a black crown and white below. In the breeding season the white nape turns black. On the bill, the lower mandible is much longer than the upper and both are red tipped with black. Long, broad wings and red legs and feet. The female is much smaller than the male

HABITAT Lagoons, estuaries, salt marshes, and coasts

SIMILAR SPECIES Quite unique as no other bird has a lower mandible that is longer than the upper

RAZORBILL (ALCA TORDA)

SIZE 17 inches

DESCRIPTION Plumage is black above and white below and in the breeding season has a thin, white line from the eye to the bill. Large head with short, thickset neck. Bill is short and black with a white band near the tip. Tail is long and pointed – it is often held pointed upward when swimming

HABITAT Offshore, rocky ground, and cliffs

SIMILAR SPECIES Similar to the Thick-billed Murre but has a shorter neck and a thicker bill with the distinctive white band

The Razorbill feeds on fish, squid, and shrimp and is capable of diving 60 feet below the surface of the water to search for food. It nests in colonies using boulders or rocky cliffs to lay the eggs on the ground or on a ledge. A single blue-green, dark-spotted egg is incubated by both parents for about 5–6 weeks. The young chick is able to leave the nest after 2 weeks but remains with the adults for some time. Juveniles are very similar to adults but lack the white bill band. The Razorbill is a seabird that lives on the Atlantic coast and can always be found in Newfoundland venturing as far north as Greenland in the summer and down to North Carolina in the winter.

(CEPPHUS GRYLLE) BLACK GUILLEMOT

The Black Guillemot nests in colonies using rocky shores and will find crevices in the rocks to lay 1–2 greenish, dark-spotted or dull white eggs. Both adults incubate the eggs for 3–4 weeks with the young leaving the nest after another 5–6 weeks, but remaining with the parents for some time. The juvenile has similar plumage to the winter adult but with a more mottled head and black edges on the white underwings. It feeds on squid, mollusks, shrimps, and fish and can often be observed sitting on open rocks. This guillemot is quite a common bird that can be seen in the north, northeast and northwest Alaska, tending to remain near land, especially in the breeding season.

SIZE 13 inches
DESCRIPTION Broad, rounded wings and red feet. The breeding bird has black plumage with a white oval patch on the upper wing. In winter it is mainly black with heavy black mottling on the back and a whitish-colored head
HABITAT Offshore and rocky shores
SIMILAR SPECIES Very similar to the Pigeon Guillemot but in the breeding season this bird will show a dark bar that extends into the wing patch. The Pigeon Guillemot also has dark wing linings that can be seen in flight whereas the Black Guillemot has white underwings with black edges

ATLANTIC PUFFIN
(FRATERCULA ARCTICA)

The Atlantic Puffin feeds on fish, mollusks, and crustaceans, diving under water to find its catch. In the winter these birds leave their breeding colonies and remain at sea. In the summer the Atlantic Puffin nests in large colonies on offshore islands. The single white egg is laid at the end of a soft burrow in the earth and is incubated by both parents for 5–6 weeks. Both are involved in feeding the chick and are able to carry copious amounts of small fish in their massive bills. After about 40 days the parents leave the chick to fend for itself. Without any food it waits for up to 10 days as its plumage grows and then, in the safety of darkness, the puffin makes its way down to the sea.

SIZE 12½ inches
DESCRIPTION Very large multi-colored bill. Black cap and upper parts with white underneath. Orange legs and webbed feet. In winter the face is gray with a smaller and more dull-colored bill. The juvenile is similar in appearance but with a smaller, darker bill
HABITAT Offshore
SIMILAR SPECIES Similar to the Horned Puffin which is only found on the Pacific Coast

TUFTED PUFFIN (FRATERCULA CIRRHATA)

SIZE 15 inches

DESCRIPTION Large round head with a short neck with a large orange-red parrot-type bill. Large red-webbed feet. In the breeding season it is black with a white face and a long yellow tuft that droops from behind the eye. In the winter the face becomes black and the tuft is less distinctive. The bill sheds several of the brightly colored cover plates that re-grow the following spring and becomes smaller and more dull

HABITAT Rocky coasts and offshore

SIMILAR SPECIES The winter adult and juvenile resemble the Rhinoceros Auklet but with thicker, more orange-red bills and more rounded heads

The Tufted Puffin spends the winters out at sea but in summer returns to the coast to nest in huge, dense colonies on vertical sea cliffs. Each pair produces a single white-blue and sometimes spotted egg in the crevice of a rock or at the end of a burrow in soft earth that might be up to 7 feet long. Very little is known about the incubation or nesting period. The juvenile resembles the winter adult but has a smaller, duller bill and is white underneath – it will take several years to achieve full adult plumage. It feeds on fish which are caught offshore during the day, supplemented with crustaceans and mollusks. It is widespread and common along the Pacific coast of North America.

(COLUMBA LIVIA) ROCK DOVE

The Rock Dove feeds on grain, seeds, fruit, and bread. These birds originated from the Atlantic and Mediterranean coasts but were domesticated all over the world for their meat and to carry messages. Many escaped and their descendants have formed feral flocks. It builds an untidy nest of grass and sticks on a sheltered ledge in a building or on a cliff or occasionally in a tree where 1–2 white eggs are laid. After 2–3 weeks' incubation the chicks remain in the nest for about 7 weeks. The adults begin to breed in March and produce several broods. Both parents share the incubation and the care of the young that are fed on regurgitated "pigeon's milk", a secretion from the bird's crop.

Size 12½ inches

Description The domestic pigeon: its most common plumage is blue-gray with a darker head and iridescent green-purple on the neck. White rump, a dark band at the end of the tail and two dark bars along the wings. However, breeders have developed several color strains and these birds vary considerably

Habitat Cities, towns, and farms

Similar Species The feral Rock Dove has a wide variety of colors and can look very similar to the wild native species

MOURNING DOVE
(ZENAIDA MACROURA)

SIZE 12 inches

DESCRIPTION A slender bird with narrow, pointed wings and a long tail with black edging to the side feathers and tipped with white. Eyes have light blue rings and there is a dark spot at the base of the ear. Plumage is pale gray-brown with black spots on the wings and buff underparts. The male has a pinkish chest and iridescent gray-blue on the crown but the female is plainer in color with a shorter tail

HABITAT Woodlands, farms, urban areas, and open brushland

SIMILAR SPECIES The juvenile resembles the Inca or Common Ground-dove but lacks the rust-colored wings

The Mourning Dove name comes from the male's rather mournful cry which sounds similar to an owl. The Mourning Dove is a common bird throughout the United States and can be seen in Canada in the summer. It constructs a flimsy nest of twigs and sticks in a tree or a bush before laying 2 white eggs. The adults alternate incubation for 2 weeks and once hatched the chicks remain in the nest for a further 16 days with both parents feeding them regurgitated food. They are then weaned onto insects before eating a full adult diet of seeds and grain. There are usually 2–4 broods in a season and the juveniles are very similar to adults but with more scaling.

YELLOW-BILLED CUCKOO
(COCCYZUS AMERICANUS)

The Yellow-billed Cuckoo builds small, loosely constructed nests from twigs about 10 feet from the ground and lays 2–4 blue-green eggs that both parents incubate for 2 weeks. The chicks are naked when they hatch and the feathers take about 6 days to begin to appear. The young then leave the nest 2 weeks after hatching. Juveniles lack the yellow bill and have an undertail that is browner with less contrast. It eats berries and insects, particularly liking hairy caterpillars which are not popular with other birds. This cuckoo is common in woodland in summer but not easy to spot as it hides in dense foliage. The population is decreasing is its natural habitat is beginning to disappear.

SIZE 12 inches

DESCRIPTION Slim bird with slender bill that curves down slightly with a yellow lower mandible and a yellow ring surrounding the eye. Gray-brown plumage above with white below and a black undertail that has white spots. In flight white underwings are edged with rust and are gray-brown above with rust patches

HABITAT Trees by lowland rivers and open woods

SIMILAR SPECIES Adult is distinctive but juvenile is similar to Black-billed Cuckoo

GREATER ROADRUNNER
(GEOCOCCYX CALIFORNIANUS)

The Great Roadrunner is actually a ground-dwelling cuckoo. It is a very fast runner, often achieving speeds of 15 miles an hour. This speed enables it to catch a wide variety of food including snakes, lizards, rodents, small birds, and large insects. Most are caught in the bill and swallowed whole although larger catches may be beaten on a rock to soften them. It is most commonly found in the deserts of the southwest but also across much of southern America. The Great Roadrunner builds small, immaculate nests in mesquite or cactus where 3–6 white eggs are laid. After 3 weeks' incubation the young hatch at intervals and are fed by both parents, remaining in the nest for another 2–3 weeks.

SIZE 23 inches
DESCRIPTION Large bird with a bushy crest, a dark heavy bill and a long tail with white edges. Brown plumage with a green sheen streaked with black and white above and buff undersides with brown streaks on the breast
HABITAT Mesquite groves and scrub desert
SIMILAR SPECIES Very distinctive bird

BURROWING OWL
(SPEOTYTO CUNICULARIA)

The Burrowing Owl can be observed standing on fence posts or on the ground. It preys on small rodents and large insects generally hunting during the day, but the male also goes out at night when sourcing food for the young chicks. It nests in the abandoned burrows of prairie dogs or ground squirrels in the west or the gopher turtle in Florida. Typically the burrow will slope down for around 3 feet before running horizontally for approximately 10 feet from the entrance. At the end of this is the nesting chamber that the owls line with grass, dried mammal dung, feathers, and the remains of prey. Five to seven white eggs are laid and incubated for about 4 weeks with both parents sharing incubation and rearing.

SIZE 9½ inches
DESCRIPTION A small owl with long legs and a short, stubby tail. The head is flat and the eyes are yellow. Brown plumage with white spots above and on the upper breast with a white throat and eyebrows. Brown and white barring below
HABITAT Prairies, deserts, and open country
SIMILAR SPECIES The long legs make it distinctive

BARN OWL
(TYTO ALBA)

The Barn Owl is nocturnal and will hunt for mice, voles, and rats, taking its prey back to the nesting site. Roosts are chosen in well-hidden corners of old buildings or tree holes and cliff edges as the bird's white plumage makes camouflage difficult. It returns to the same breeding site each year and lay 5–11 white eggs on a bare surface, with incubation carried out by the female for 5 weeks while the male feeds her. Although the young are ready to leave the nest at about 8 weeks it is normally 12 weeks before they are fully independent. Although widespread, the Barn Owl population is declining and this bird is now becoming quite a rare sight in North America.

Size 16 inches
Description White heart-shaped face edged with tan with large brown eyes. Sandy brown plumage flecked with gray and brown with white underparts. Long feathered legs. Females are darker than males
Habitat Trees, cliffs, barns and old buildings
Similar Species The Snowy Owl is whiter with a smaller head and yellow eyes

LONG-EARED OWL (ASIO OTUS)

SIZE 15 inches

DESCRIPTION Quite a slender owl with buff or rust-colored facial discs and a dark stripe through the eyes that are orange-yellow in color. Long ear tufts positioned close together. Gray-brown plumage above and whitish below with dark vertical streaks

HABITAT Dense woods

SIMILAR SPECIES Similar to the Great Horned Owl but is smaller and less bulky and lacks the white throat and horizontal barring

The Long-eared Owl lives in dense woods and with its excellent camouflage and nocturnal habits can be very hard to spot. It is fairly uncommon but may be seen in small flocks during the winter. It does not construct its own nest but uses instead the nest already built by a crow, squirrel, or magpie. This owl will lay 3–8 white eggs before the existing inhabitants are ready to breed thus forcing them out to build elsewhere. The female usually incubates the eggs for about 4 weeks and the young chicks are ready to leave 5 weeks after hatching. It hunts for rodents and can sometimes be mobbed by smaller birds although it is rare for it to attack them.

(ASIO FLAMMEUS) SHORT-EARED OWL

The Short-eared Owl is a common bird which can sometimes be seen in small flocks in the winter. It uses a well-hidden, grass-lined depression in the ground to lay its 5–9 creamy-white eggs. The female produces these every 1 to 2 days with incubation taking approximately 21 days in total. The young are ready to leave the nest a further 6 weeks later. This owl hunts predominantly at dusk and at night preying on small mammals such as meadow voles, shrews, and moles. These are caught by hovering over the ground to locate the animal prior to pouncing but occasionally they pinpoint it from a convenient perch or while standing on the ground.

SIZE 15 inches

DESCRIPTION This owl has pale facial discs with black around the yellow-colored eyes. Short ear tufts although these are not easy to see. Mottled brownish plumage above and buff below with brown vertical streaking. When in flight the pale linings of the wings and a dark patch at the wrist with a buff patch above, can be seen

HABITAT Tundra, brushy areas, marshes, dunes, prairies, fields, and open ground

SIMILAR SPECIES Resembles the Long-eared Owl which is darker with longer ears

GREAT HORNED OWL
(BUBO VIRGINIANUS)

The Great Horned Owl will use a nest abandoned by a heron, hawk, or crow, located in a tree, rocky crevice, or on a cliff ledge. The female lays 2–4 white eggs and incubates them for 7 weeks, but both parents feed the young after hatching and the chicks are ready to leave the nest 10 weeks later. It is a powerful bird with a sharp, hooked bill and long talons, and a voracious appetite. This owl will therefore hunt for large prey such as squirrels, rabbits, snakes, skunks, and geese. Most of this takes place at night but it might also be observed during the day when it is frequently mobbed by smaller birds. The Great Horned Owl is the most widespread owl in North America.

SIZE 22 inches
DESCRIPTION A large bird with widely spaced ear tufts making it resemble a cat. The eyes are yellow and the plumage mottled brown-gray above, with a white throat and horizontal barring below that is dark gray
HABITAT Woodlands, desert, and urban areas
SIMILAR SPECIES Resembles the Long-eared Owl but is larger and more bulky and has the white throat and vertical streaks on the undersides

EASTERN SCREECH-OWL (OTUS ASIO)

Size 8½ inches

Description A small owl with a yellow-green bill tipped with white and small ear tufts that stand out when raised but are often held flat against the head. Plumage varies considerably from gray through to brown or rust but they usually have vertical streaks on the undersides crossed with widely-spaced dark bars

Habitat Forest, farmlands, parks, and towns

Similar Species There are three Screech-owls and all are similar. The Whiskered is slightly smaller with bolder bars on the undersides while the Western Screech-owl is usually gray and has a dark bill

The Eastern Screech-owl nests in tree cavities, often using nesting boxes or old woodpecker holes. Its 4–6 white eggs are mainly incubated by the female with the male protecting the nest and hunting for food. The downy chicks remain in the nest for 4 weeks after hatching. The Eastern Screech-owl is a nocturnal bird that hunts for mice and insects, occasionally diving for fish. It is common throughout its range, but due to the excellent camouflage, its small size and nocturnal activity, it is very difficult to spot. The call is a mellow hoot or a quavery, eerie wail. Preferring large trees, it can often live undetected in parks or mature back yards.

(NYCTEA SCANDIACA) SNOWY OWL

The Snowy Owl breeds on tundra, finding a depression to line with moss and grass. The female incubates the 5–9 eggs for 4–5 weeks and the young are ready to leave the nest about 6 weeks after hatching. Juveniles and adult females are basically white but with great variation in the amount of black spotting and barring, while the adult male is almost pure white. Hunting takes place during the day or night. The Snowy Owl's main diet consists of lemmings, but it will also prey on birds and small mammals, and eat carrion. It is an Arctic bird but as it is so heavily dependent on the lemming, it will move south whenever the lemming population falls.

SIZE 23 inches

DESCRIPTION Large owl with yellow eyes and small head. Adult male is almost pure white while juveniles and adult females are basically white but with great variation in the amount of black spotting and barring

HABITAT Open fields, tundra, prairies, and marshes

SIMILAR SPECIES The Barn Owl is similar but has dark eyes and a heart-shaped face. The young of other owls are also white at first

GREAT GRAY OWL
(STRIX NEBULOSA)

The Great Gray Owl preys predominantly on mice but will also hunt for birds and small mammals. Although mainly nocturnal it will also hunt at dusk and dawn and even during the day in the far north where daylight hours are very long. It is the largest owl in North America and is relatively uncommon. Its size, however, can be deceptive as it is covered in a very large layer of feathers to provide the bird with insulation for the cold climate in which it lives. The Great Gray Owl lays 2–5 white eggs in the nest of another bird sited in a tree or on a cliff. The female incubates them for 4–5 weeks and the chicks leave the nest about 5 weeks after hatching.

SIZE 27 inches

DESCRIPTION Large owl with a large head and big, pale facial disks that have concentric gray circles patterned on them. The eyes and bill are yellow and the tail is long. Mottled gray-brown plumage above with subtle gray vertical streaks below. Black spot on the chin and two white neck markings

HABITAT Dense coniferous forests, wooded bogs, and boreal forests

SIMILAR SPECIES Size and color make this owl distinctive

COMMON NIGHTHAWK
(CHORDEILES MINOR)

SIZE 9½ in

DESCRIPTION Slender, long wings; mottled black-brown above, paler beneath, dusky barring, white across wing; male has white throat and tail band; slightly forked tail

HABITAT Woodland, farmland, and suburbs

SIMILAR SPECIES Lesser Nighthawk is paler, has more rounded wings, pale wing bar is nearer the tip of wing

The Common Nighthawk glides and flies high above the ground, its rather erratic wingbeats interspersed with easier strokes, catching insects. The male makes display flights on warm summer evenings, diving steeply. Despite the name it is not a hawk. Common across much of its range, numbers are now declining. It winters in the subtropics, including parts of Mexico. No nest is built; the 2 eggs are laid directly on a flat roof or the ground. They are incubated by the female for 20 days or so and both parents feed the chicks until they are able to leave about 3 weeks later. Birds in the east tend to be browner in color while northern birds are grayer; both the female and the juvenile have a buff-colored throat and wing bar.

WHIP-POOR-WILL
(CAPRIMULGUS VOCIFERUS)

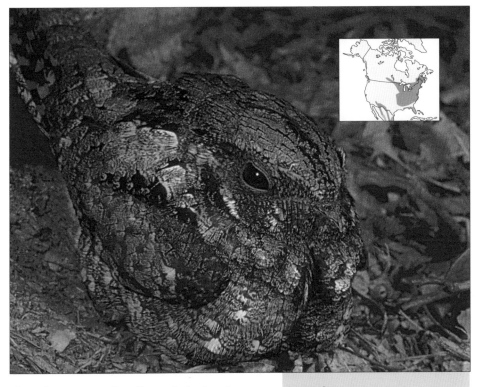

The Whip-poor-will will search for beetles, moths, and other large insects by gliding close to the forest floor with its mouth wide open to catch them in flight. This night bird's call echoes its own name but it is very difficult to use this sound to locate this elusive bird. During the day the Whip-poor-will sits or sleeps on the forest floor using its excellent camouflage for protection. It lays eggs among the leaves on the forest floor. Producing 2 whitish eggs with random brown or gray spots, the female will incubate them for 3 weeks and the young chicks leave the nest a further 2–3 weeks after hatching.

SIZE 9¾ inches

DESCRIPTION Mottled gray-brown-black plumage and a white throat with black necklace markings. Large dark eyes, rounded wings and a long, rounded tail with outer tail feathers that are white on the male and buff on the female

HABITAT Deciduous and mixed woods with clearings

SIMILAR SPECIES Similar to the Chuck-will's–widow that is bigger and redder in color with a whitish band above the black breast

CHIMNEY SWIFT
(CHAETURA PELAGICA)

Originally the Chimney Swift used hollow trees to nest but now finds buildings such as chimneys or barns. The neat cup-shaped nest is made using twigs glued together with saliva and is where 4–5 white eggs are laid. Both parents incubate them and the young leave after 4 weeks. Days are spent in flight either beating the wings rapidly or holding them stiffly in a glide as it continually searches for insects in the air. This bird been described as "like a cigar with wings" and emits a very distinctive call of rapid chippering notes. At night it will cling to a vertical wall to roost. Summers are spent all over eastern America before migrating to the rainforests in South America for the winter.

Size 5¼ inches

Description A small bird with a short and rather stubby-looking tail. Long, curved, narrow wings and a slim body with sooty brown plumage and a paler throat

Habitat Farmlands, woodlands, towns, and cities

Similar Species Resembles Vaux's Swift but is slightly larger and darker on the rump and breast

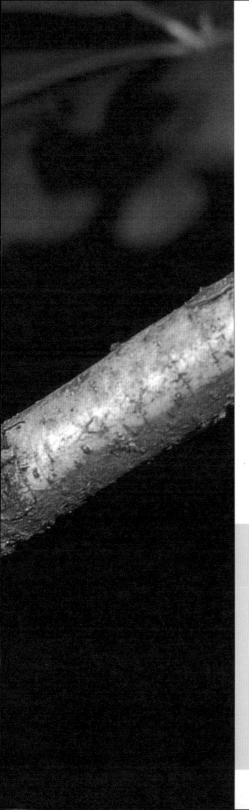

RUBY-THROATED HUMMINGBIRD
(ARCHILOCHUS COLUBRIS)

The Ruby-throated Hummingbird is a very anti-social bird, only seen in pairs during the breeding season. It prefers nectar from red tubular flowers and supplements this with small spiders and tiny flying insects. Found in the east in the summer it migrates across the Gulf of Mexico to winter in Central America. It builds a nest from plant down and spiders' webs. Two white eggs are laid that the female incubates for 11–14 days. The young take 2–4 weeks to leave the nest and the female raises 2–3 clutches on her own. The male defends the breeding area and the resources of nectar, exhibiting spectacular displays. The female defends the nest in the breeding season but at other times also defends the nectar resources.

SIZE 3¾ inches

DESCRIPTION The male has a metallic green back, an iridescent scarlet or ruby throat and a black face and chin. The tail is dark and completely forked. The female and immature bird has a white chin and throat with thin dark streaks, a dark tail with a shallow fork and white tips to the outer tail feathers

HABITAT Deciduous and mixed forest, and yards

SIMILAR SPECIES All female hummingbirds are very similar. The male is similar to the male Broad-tailed Hummingbird which has a more rose-colored throat

RUFOUS HUMMINGBIRD
(SELASPHORUS RUFUS)

Size 3¾ inches

Description A small bird with short wings. The male has a rufous back and sides with a bright orange-red throat and white breast. The female has a green back, rufous sides, an orange-red spotted throat patch with white beneath. Outer tail feathers are white at the tip, black in the middle and rufous at the base. Juveniles are similar to females

Habitat Edges of woodlands, and alpine meadows

Similar Species Male has very distinctive markings. Juvenile resembles juvenile male Allen's Hummingbird. The female is similar to the female Broad-tailed hummingbird but has a reddish throat patch and a shorter tail. Also resembles the female Allen's but has less rufous coloring in the tail

The Rufous Hummingbird uses plant down to weave a cup-shaped nest decorated with moss and lichen. This is attached to a branch where the female incubates 2 white eggs with the young leaving the nest 3 weeks after hatching. Both sexes fiercely defend their territory and the nectar resources, supplementing this staple diet with running tree sap and tiny flying insects. A whistling buzz can sometimes be heard when the bird is in flight. Flying further north than any hummingbird, it is found along the Pacific coast in summer and over the east during the fall when it migrates to the south. Some remain along the Gulf coast in the winter but the majority fly on to southern Mexico.

CALLIOPE HUMMINGBIRD
(STELLULA CALLIOPE)

The Calliope Hummingbird feeds on nectar, small insects, and spiders. It is the smallest bird in North America and is common across the northwest in summer where it can be found in mountain meadows. Migration takes place across the southwest as this bird winters in Mexico. It uses moss and lichen to construct a cup-shaped nest that is decorated with spider web and attached to a sheltered branch of a tree or bush. After 2 white eggs are laid the female incubates them for 2 weeks with the young leaving the nest 3 weeks after hatching. The juvenile resembles the female but has some additional red markings on the throat by the end of the summer.

SIZE 3¼ inches

DESCRIPTION A tiny bird with a thin bill and a short tail. The male has metallic green plumage above, a white throat with purple-violet streaks, and a whitish breast. The female has green plumage above with white undersides and dark streaks on the throat. The flanks are buff-colored and outer tail feathers are tipped with white

HABITAT Mountain meadows

SIMILAR SPECIES The streaks on the throat make the male distinctive. Juveniles resemble juvenile Allen's and Broad-tailed Hummingbirds. Female resembles female Rufous and Broad-tailed Hummingbirds but is smaller in size and has less rufous on the tail

BELTED KINGFISHER
(CERYLE ALCYON)

SIZE 13 inches

DESCRIPTION A medium size bird with a heavy bill and a shaggy crest. Blue-gray plumage above and on the head with a white collar. Both males and females have a blue-gray breast band and white on the belly while the female also has a rust-red band on the belly. Both have white underwings and blue-gray along the trailing edge that can be seen in flight

HABITAT Ponds, streams, coasts, shores of lakes, and estuaries

SIMILAR SPECIES Male is distinctive. The female resembles the female Ringed Kingfisher but is smaller with white and rust on the belly and white underwings

The Belted Kingfisher digs a tunnel measuring up to 7 feet long in the sides of a steep riverbank and deposits its 5–8 white eggs on bare earth at the end of the tunnel. These are incubated for 3–4 weeks. The young are fully fledged before they leave the burrow at around 7 weeks. It feeds on fish, frogs, tadpoles, and insects and will hunt by perching on a branch over water looking for food, then hovering over the water before it dives. A common bird, the Belted Kingfisher is the only kingfisher to be found across most of North America and is quite easy to spot near water. It is a solitary creature that defends its fishing territory and only pairs up during the breeding season.

DOWNY WOODPECKER
(PICOIDES PUBESCENS)

The smallest North American woodpecker, the Downy Woodpecker is common across the continent except in the north and southwest. It prefers to excavate nesting holes up to 50 feet from the ground in dead tree trunks or branches. It lays 4–7 white eggs which are incubated by both parents for 2 weeks. Young birds leave the nest 3 weeks after hatching. It has a sharply contrasting plumage of black and white and the slightly larger male has a red patch on its nape. The amount of white spotting on the black wings can vary from region to region, in the Pacific northwest, southwest and south, less white is seen. Birds in the Pacific northwest are often more grey brown than black, but otherwise identical. They are also larger in areas of high elevation. It feeds on wood boring insects, berries and seeds, but will also come to bird tables for suet.

SIZE 6¾ inches

DESCRIPTION Smaller woodpecker with a short bill. Black crown and eye stripe on a white face. Males have a red patch on the nape. White breast and underparts, and a white back. Wings and tail are black with white spots on the wings

HABITAT Woodland, suburban gardens, parks and orchards

SIMILAR SPECIES Hairy Woodpecker which is almost identical but larger with a longer bill. Other small black and white woodpeckers have proportionally longer bills

HAIRY WOODPECKER
(PICOIDES VILLOSUS)

Common across most of the continent, the Hairy Woodpecker is found in woodland where large and dead trees are found. It also frequents gardens and residential areas. It drills cavities for nesting high above the ground and often uses the same hole for several years. Four to seven white eggs are laid which are incubated by both parents, the male at night and the female during the day for two weeks. Fledglings leave the nest 4–5 weeks later. The white patch on its black back and the white eyebrow streak mark it out from other black and white woodpeckers, with the exception of the Downy Woodpecker. The male has a distinctive red patch on the nape, whereas the female is black. Birds found in the Pacific north-west tend to be more dark gray than black, but are otherwise the same. Although it eats some vegetable matter, it feeds mainly on insects often boring deep into bark to obtain its prey. Its tendency to eat insect pests makes it a valuable asset to most woodlands areas. The Hairy Woodpecker engages in displays during mating and to show aggression. It drums on trees to proclaim its territory.

Size 9¼ inches

Description Medium-sized woodpecker with a long bill. A black and white striped head, white back, breast and underparts, black wings, rump and tail. The wings are marked with white spots. The male has a red patch on the nape

Habitat Open woodland and more dense mature forests

Similar Species Almost identical to the Downy Woodpecker, which is smaller with a shorter bill

RED-HEADED WOODPECKER
(MELANERPES ERYTHROCEPHALUS)

SIZE 9¼ inches

DESCRIPTION A medium-sized bird that has blue-black plumage on the back and pure white undersides. The head, neck, and throat are bright red. Large white wing patches and a white rump are visible in flight

HABITAT Groves, swamps with dead trees, open and dense woods

SIMILAR SPECIES A distinctive and unmistakable bird

The Red-headed Woodpecker pecks at tree bark to feed on beetles and insects, supplemented with insects caught in mid-air, acorns, and nuts. Often this species will store food in crevices or knotholes for future use. It is a common bird but in certain areas the population is beginning to decline due to loss of breeding habitat and competition for nesting holes from birds such as starlings. It finds dead wood to excavate a hole where it lays 4–6 white eggs. Both adults incubate the clutch for about 14 days and the young leave the nest about 4 weeks after hatching, with a second brood often being produced. The juvenile is duller in color with dark bars across the wing patch and a brownish head.

YELLOW-BELLIED SAPSUCKER
(SPHYRAPICUS VARIUS)

A fully migratory woodpecker, the Yellow-bellied Sapsucker moves south toward the southeastern United States and into South America as far as Panama. Like woodpeckers, sapsuckers drill holes in trees in search of insects, but they are also boring for the sap which oozes out, returning regularly to drink. They often drill sap holes in rows. Breeding pairs will bore a hole up to 45 feet from the ground in a dead trunk or branch where 4–6 white eggs are laid. These are incubated for 12 days by both parents and the young leave the nest 4 weeks after hatching. Juvenile birds remain brown until after their first winter, but have a reddish wash on their forehead. The adult male can be distinguished from the female by its bright red throat, the female's is white.

SIZE 8½ inches
DESCRIPTION Medium-sized, slender woodpecker with long wings. A black and white striped head, red forehead, black back and wings marked with white bars. Yellow breast which fades to creamy white underparts. Male has red chin and throat, female white
HABITAT Forest and woodland, mainly deciduous
SIMILAR SPECIES Similar to the Red-naped Sapsucker which has a red patch on the back of the neck

NORTHERN FLICKER (COLAPTES AURATUS)

SIZE 12½ inches

DESCRIPTION Large woodpecker with broad wings and long tail. Back and wings are brown barred with black. Lighter brown breast and belly are heavily spotted with black and breast has a black crescent bib. Face color either brown or gray depending on color-form

HABITAT Open woodland, forest edges, and suburban yards

SIMILAR SPECIES The Gilded Flicker has yellow underwings unlike the "red-shafted." It also lacks a red patch on the nape like the "yellow-shafted"

The Northern Flicker exists in two color-forms. The "yellow-shafted" flicker is found to the east of the continent and has yellow wing and tail linings, most obvious in flight. It has a grey crown with a red patch on the nape, a tan face and a black mustache. The "red-shafted" flicker, to the west, has pale red underwing and undertail linings. Its crown is brown with no red on the nape and its face is gray with a red mustache. Where they overlap, they interbreed, producing many variations. Unlike other woodpeckers the Northern Flicker is unable to drill into hard trees and so relies upon soft and dead trees for nesting. Breeding pairs excavate nesting holes in trees, fence posts, or cactus high above the ground in order to lay 5–10 white eggs which hatch after 12 days. It forages on the ground for food such as ants and insects and eats berries in winter.

(EMPIDONAX MINIMUS) LEAST FLYCATCHER

One of the most common flycatchers in North America, the Least Flycatcher is found across the north of the continent during summer before migrating to the Southern Hemisphere. It breeds up to 60 feet from the ground on a tree branch, building its nest from woven plant fibers. Three to five white eggs are laid which are incubated for up to 2 weeks and the young leave the nest after 14 days. It feeds on winged insects which it catches in flight, returning to its perch to consume its prey. Since empidonax flycatchers are difficult to tell apart by sight, the song is useful for identification; it has a dry call with a snappy *che-bec* song.

SIZE 5¼ inches

DESCRIPTION Small body, short wings, triangular head and bill. Upperparts are olive gray, whitish throat, pale gray breast and yellow-white underparts. Wings and tail are dark brown with two white bars on wing. White eye ring

HABITAT Open, deciduous woodland, parks, and orchards

SIMILAR SPECIES All empidonax flycatchers are difficult to tell apart and are mainly distinguished by their habitat, range, and voice

WESTERN WOOD-PEWEE
(CONTOPUS SORDIDULUS)

Size 6¼ inches

Description Medium-sized flycatcher with a long slender body, wings, and tail. Dark, olive-gray upperparts, pale gray underparts with yellow wash to chin and belly. Two pale buff wingbars

Habitat Open woodland, wooded canyons, and rivers

Similar Species Almost identical to Eastern Wood-pewee, distinguished only by range. Lacks the pale eye ring of similar empidonax flycatchers

A relatively plain bird, the Western Wood-pewee is common throughout the west of North America. For the winter it migrates further south. It lays 3–4 creamy white eggs marked with purple-brown spots in a well camouflaged nest constructed of plant fibers. The eggs are incubated by the female for 1–2 weeks and the young leave the nest 15–19 days after hatching. It feeds almost exclusively on insects although it will also eat berries. Flies are caught in the air and the bird will maintain a high hunting perch in order to locate its prey. Its song can usually be heard at dawn and dusk and consists of a soft *beeer* whistle.

BLACK PHOEBE
(SAYORNIS NIGRICANS)

A territorial and solitary bird, the Black Phoebe is almost always found near to water where it can feed on the abundance of insects. Although non-breeding birds may wander, the majority will remain in the same area throughout the year. Nests of mud, moss, and grass are attached to crevices under canopies such as ledges, bridges, or riverside tree roots. The female lays 3–6 white eggs with faint brown spots and these are incubated for 15–17 days. The young leave the nest after 2–3 weeks to make way for a second brood. Juvenile birds tend to be dark gray-brown. Its posture is distinctive as it perches erect, bobbing, wagging, and fanning its tail.

SIZE 6¾ inches

DESCRIPTION Medium-sized, slender flycatcher with long wings and tail and a peaked head. Eye, bill and plumage is slate black, except for belly and undertail which are pure white

HABITAT Shady wooded areas near to water

SIMILAR SPECIES Coloring and habits make it distinctive

VERMILION FLYCATCHER
(PYROCEPHALUS RUBINUS)

A distinctive and striking flycatcher which is common within its limited range. It is easy to observe as it perches low on shrubs and bushes, often bobbing its tail like a phoebe. Breeding birds build open-cup nests out of twigs, stems, and plant material, under a natural canopy in woodland. The female lays 2 or 3 white eggs with lilac blotches which she incubates for 2 weeks. Fledglings leave the nest after 2 weeks and a second brood follows. Juvenile birds are similar to the female in coloring, but with more spotting and streaking on the breast. It feeds almost exclusively on insects which it catches in flight.

SIZE 6 inches

DESCRIPTION Medium-sized, short tailed with short bill. Male has bright red cap, throat, and underparts. Black eye stripe, back, wings and tail. Female has gray-brown upperparts, black tail, white forehead, eyebrow, and breast and pinkish underparts

HABITAT Streams and ponds, requires woodland near water for breeding

SIMILAR SPECIES Male is unmistakable, color of female and juvenile are distinctive

EASTERN KINGBIRD (TYRANNUS TYRANNUS)

SIZE 8½ inches

DESCRIPTION Medium-sized with large head and narrow, pointed wings. Head and back is almost black, throat, chest and belly are white. White tip on blackish tail. Slightly crested head conceals red-orange feathers, rarely seen

HABITAT Open areas, woodland clearings, agricultural land, forest edges

SIMILAR SPECIES White tail band and black and white plumage distinguish it from other kingbirds

The Eastern Kingbird can often be seen perching on treetops, fence posts, and utility poles from the Atlantic to the Pacific. It is highly territorial and will aggressively defend its area from other birds. Its nest is bulky, made out of twigs, roots, and grass usually high in a tree. Three to five white eggs are laid which are incubated by the female for 2 weeks. Although fledglings leave the nest after 2 weeks, they continue to be fed by the parents for up to 7 weeks, and only one brood is produced. Juvenile birds have brownish gray upperparts and a darker breast, they also lack the white tail band. It feeds on insects caught in flight, but will also eat berries.

(LANIUS LUDOVICIANUS) LOGGERHEAD SHRIKE

Fairly common, although its numbers are in decline in certain areas, the Loggerhead Shrike is a hunting songbird. It catches its prey, including large insects and mice, lizards and small birds and impales them upon thorns or barbed wire in order to kill and eat. Its tendency to store excess food in this way often marks its presence. It builds nests of twigs and feathers above the ground in trees or bushes and lays 3–8 greenish white eggs which are incubated by the female for 16 days. The young leave the nest 3 weeks after hatching. Juvenile birds are paler with faint barring above and below.

SIZE 9 inches

DESCRIPTION Medium-sized, long wings, long tail, small head. Dark hooked bill. Blue gray above, white below. Black eye mask, wings and tail. White throat, rump and outer tail feathers, white wing patches

HABITAT Open countryside

SIMILAR SPECIES The Northern Shrike is slightly larger, with an eye mask that does not meet above the bill and is paler in color. Northern Mockingbirds lack the black mask

YELLOW-THROATED VIREO
(VIREO FLAVIFRONS)

SIZE 5½ inches

DESCRIPTION Stocky with large head. Olive head and back, gray rump, dark wings and tail. Yellow throat and breast, white belly and two white wing bars. Dark eye encircled with bold yellow spectacles

HABITAT Oak and mixed woods, groves with tall hardwood trees

SIMILAR SPECIES Pine Warbler has similar plumage but with streaked sides and lacks eye ring. Juvenile White-eyed Vireo lacks the yellow throat

Common during the summer months throughout the east of North America, the Yellow-throated Vireo migrates to the Southern Hemisphere in fall. It prefers to remain high up in trees where it forages for food, mainly insects although it does eat fruit and berries. Following a courtship ritual which involves the male selecting a nest site, the female builds a cup nest and lays 3–5 white eggs with lilac-brown blotches. Both parents incubate the eggs for 2 weeks, the young leave the nest 14 days after hatching. Juveniles are duller than the adult with less dark eyes. Adults remain solitary outside the breeding season and form a pair only long enough to produce a brood.

RED-EYED VIREO
(VIREO OLIVACEUS)

Although common during the summer months, the Red-eyed Vireo is more often heard than seen, since it prefers to remain high in the forest canopy. It feeds mainly on insects and relies upon fruit and berries during winter before migration. Cup nests of twigs, plant fibers, and spider webs are suspended from tree branches up to 60 feet from the ground. These hold 3–4 white eggs spotted with brown which are incubated for 12–14 days. The young leave the nest 12 days after hatching. Juvenile birds have brown eyes and a yellow wash to their undertail and flanks, a plumage which is repeated in adult birds every fall.

SIZE 6 inches

DESCRIPTION Stocky with a long, thick bill. Gray crown, olive back and wings. White underparts. White eyebrow stripe with dark border. Red eye

HABITAT Dense woodland and forest, preferably deciduous or mixed deciduous

SIMILAR SPECIES Warbling Vireo is smaller and paler

BLUE JAY
(CYANOCITTA CRISTATA)

Common and noisy, Blue Jays are often seen in urban gardens and parks and will regularly visit back yard feeders. Found across the east of North America during summer, in fall some birds migrate south in large flocks. This bird builds a bulky nest out of twigs, high up on a tree branch or crotch and lays 3–5 olive, blue or buffy eggs. These are incubated by the female for 16–18 days and fledge after a further 3 weeks. It can appropriate the nests of other birds, and will even feed from the eggs and young of other birds. However, on the whole Blue Jays eat nuts, seeds, fruit, and insects.

Size 11 inches

Description Violet-blue crest and upperparts. Gray-white throat and underparts. Black collar and eye stripe extending to beneath the back of the crest. Black barring on wings and tail with white corners

Habitat Woodland and urban areas including parks and yards

Similar species Coloring distinctive, often mimics the call of other birds

GRAY JAY (PERISOREUS CANADENSIS)

SIZE 11½ inches
DESCRIPTION Long tail and short, stocky bill.
Gray upperparts, pale gray or white
underparts. Face and forehead are white,
crown and nape can be dark gray or
brownish depending on range. Fluffy
plumage
HABITAT Mountain forests and woodland
SIMILAR SPECIES Larger than a big chickadee

A tame bird, the Gray Jay or "Canada Jay" is often spotted at woodland and mountain camp sites where it appropriates as much food as it can. It is particularly fond of carrion and will often store scraps of meats, formed into saliva-covered balls, in tree crevices and holes. It tends to remain resident in its area the year round and will breed relatively early. A bowl-shaped nest of twigs lined with feathers and hair is built up to 30 feet in a tree. It lays 3–5 green-gray spotted eggs, which the female incubates for 17–18 days. The young leave the nest 2 weeks later. Juvenile birds are much darker gray all over, with a whitish mustachial streak.

(CYANOCITTA STELLERI) STELLER'S JAY

The largest of the North American jays, Steller's Jay covers a wide range and is both common and conspicuous. These birds are often seen traveling together in small groups. It builds a sturdy bowl nest in a conifer and lays 3–5 green-blue spotted eggs which are incubated by the female for 16 days. Adult birds can display a variety of subtle markings depending upon the location. Birds in the northwest and Pacific coastal areas may have light blue and white forehead feathers and throat streaks; those found in the interior have a blacker head, with white streaks in the crest. It feeds on nuts, fruit, seeds, and insects and even the contents of other nests.

Size 11½ inches

Description Broad-winged, relatively short tail, head crest. Head and throat are black, body dark blue. Some birds have white streaks and spots on forehead and throat

Habitat Pine oak woods and coniferous forests

Similar Species Distinctive dark coloring and crest

CLARK'S NUTCRACKER

(NUCIFRAGA COLUMBIANA)

Clark's Nutcracker visits mountain camp sites and picnic spots where it scavenges for scraps of food. Its reliance upon pine seeds affects its behavior; it is frequently forced to extend its range in search of food, often toward the Pacific. It stores pine seeds in fall for winter, and uses a special pouch under its tongue to carry the seeds long distances. Storing food means it can breed early, often from January onward. The nests is an open cup and built in conifers of twigs lined with grass. The bird lays 2–6 green eggs with brown spots, which are incubated by the female and, unusually for jays, the male also for 16 days. Chicks leave the nest after 4 weeks.

SIZE 12 inches
DESCRIPTION Long wings, short tail, and a long pointed bill. Head and body has pale gray plumage. Wings and tail are black with white wing patches and white outertail feathers. Face is white, with dark eye
HABITAT Mountain woodland and coniferous forests
SIMILAR SPECIES Gray Jay has a smaller bill and lacks the white wing and tail markings

BLACK-BILLED MAGPIE (PICA PICA)

SIZE 19 inches

DESCRIPTION Sturdy body, long tail, round head. Head and body mainly black. White belly, shoulders, and wing patches. Black wings and tail have iridescent green sheen

HABITAT Open woodland, trees, thickets and suburbs

SIMILAR SPECIES Yellow-billed Magpie is smaller with a yellow bill

A common and conspicuous pied bird, the Black billed Magpie is found in both urban and rural areas, often in pairs or loose colonies. It can spend several weeks building a large bulky nest of twigs and sticks in which to lay 7–9 green-buff eggs with brown spots. These are incubated for 17 days and the young birds remain in the nest for between 23 and 32 days. Juveniles are similar in appearance to adults, but lack the iridescence. It will forage for food, including some seeds and fruit but mainly insects and carrion. The Black-billed Magpie is known to steal the eggs and chicks of other birds.

(CORVUS BRACHYRHYNCHOS) AMERICAN CROW

The American Crow is regularly seen having effectively adapted to urban environments where once it lived in woodland. An intelligent and resourceful bird, it lives in large colonies which provide protection and shared information about food sources. Family groups are often large, with relationships between family members being maintained for several years. It breeds within its colony, building a large stick nest in a tree, laying 3–8 green and brown splotched eggs. Incubation takes 17 days and the young are ready to leave after 5 weeks. Although it prefers to eat seeds, it is a predator and will eat insects, carrion, and the contents of other birds' nests. Its call is a harsh caw.

SIZE 17½ inches

DESCRIPTION Large and stocky with a short, square-ended tail and broad wings. Plumage is entirely black

HABITAT Open country, agricultural land and urban areas

SIMILAR SPECIES Fish Crow distinguished by its different call. Ravens have wedge shaped tails

COMMON RAVEN
(CORVUS CORAX)

The Common Raven is widespread across North America and in many areas is observed within cities although it prefers to avoid human contact. It can often be seen in pairs, since the bird mates for life. It soars high in the sky, riding on air currents and performing aerial acrobatics. It is primarily a scavenger, eating insects, rodents, carrion, and the contents of other nests. It also feeds on garbage. It has a deep croaking call. During the breeding season, large stick nests are built in trees and contain 4–6 light blue or green eggs with dark brown spots. The female incubates these for up to 3 weeks and the young leave the nest 5–6 weeks later.

SIZE 24 inches
DESCRIPTION Large bill, flat head, long wings. Plumage all black with purplish sheen; loose, scruffy feathers on throat. In flight wings are angular and tail is wedge shaped
HABITAT Mountains and cliffs, desert and forest
SIMILAR SPECIES Chihuahuan Raven is smaller with shorter bill and different call. American Crow has square-ended tail

HORNED LARK (EREMOPHILA ALPESTRIS)

SIZE 6¾–7¾ inches

DESCRIPTION Slender body, long wings, square tail, and stout bill. Pale brown above, white below with a black chest patch and black tail feathers. Yellow wash on face and throat, black mustache streak. Small black horns on top of head

HABITAT Open, barren country, prefers bare ground

SIMILAR SPECIES Juvenile can be confused with Sprague's Pipit

The only true lark native to North America, the Horned Lark is widespread and can often be seen gathering in large flocks during winter. It runs erratically on the ground in search of insects, grain, and seed. Its preference for barren ground has enabled it to colonize areas cultivated by humans, such as airports, which may once have been dominated by woodland. When breeding it lays 3–5 white eggs with dark spots in a grass-lined hole in the ground. The female incubates these for 11 days, and the young leave 11 days after hatching. Juvenile birds lack the adults' horns and sharp face markings and are more streaked below.

(PROGNE SUBIS) PURPLE MARTIN

The largest member of the North American swallows family. Although it is widespread, its numbers are declining in the center and west of the continent. The Purple Martin migrates south during fall to winter in South America, then returns in spring. It catches insects, such as wasps, moths, and grasshoppers, cicadas, and butterflies in flight, as well as mosquitoes. When breeding it builds a loose nest of grass, leaves, and feathers in a tree hole and lays 3–6 dull white eggs which are incubated by the female for 15–17 days. The young leave the nest after 4 weeks. Juveniles resemble the female, but with some purplish feathers on throat, breast, and flanks.

SIZE 8 inches

DESCRIPTION Large, long wings and forked tail. Male has glossy black back, black wings and tail, white chin, throat, and underparts. Female has dusky black upperparts with smoky gray throat and breast

HABITAT Prefers open countryside for breeding, savannahs, pastures, parks, and urban areas. Also found near ponds, lakes, and streams

SIMILAR SPECIES European Starling has longer bill, browner wings and lack forked tail

TREE SWALLOW
(TACHYCINETA BICOLOR)

Unlike other swallows, the Tree Swallow will eat berries in winter when insects are scarce, enabling it to winter farther north. It is also the first swallow to reappear from Central America during spring. Before migration during fall, these birds gather in enormous flocks which circle in the sky. Breeding takes place close to water and grass cup nests are made in a tree hollow. The female lays 4–6 white eggs which are incubated for 2 weeks and the young leave the nest 2–3 weeks later. Tree Swallows are less sociable during the breeding season and will forage for food alone or in loose flocks. Its preferred diet is insects caught in flight.

SIZE 5¾ inches

DESCRIPTION Stocky, broad wing, shallow forked tail. Blue-black upperparts tinged with green. Underparts are pure white from base of the bill downwards. Females are duller than males and juveniles have browner plumage with brown wash underneath

HABITAT Woodland, close to water

SIMILAR SPECIES Violet-green Swallow has a white cheek patch which extends behind the ear. Bank Swallow is similar to juvenile but with more defined breast band

BANK SWALLOW (RIPARIA RIPARIA)

Size 4¾ inches

Description A small and slender swallow with narrow wings and a long tail with slight fork. Upperparts are plain brown, underparts are pure white, with a brown band across breast

Habitat Usually found near water, breeds in sandy banks, riverbanks and gravel pits

Similar Species Northern Rough-winged Swallow is larger with a brown wash on the throat rather than a breast band

The smallest of the North American swallows, the Bank Swallow is common across North America during summer before migrating to South America in large flocks for winter. It feeds on winged insects caught in flight. It breeds in huge colonies which can number thousands, all nesting and foraging for food at the same time. It will nest in the sides of riverbanks and man-made excavations, digging deep tunnels with chambers in which to build nests made of grass and feathers. Females lay 4–6 white eggs which are incubated by both parents for 2 weeks. The young leave the nest around 3 weeks after hatching.

(HIRUNDO RUSTICA) BARN SWALLOW

Common worldwide, the Barn Swallow can be found across North America during the summer months before its migration to South America during fall. Migrating birds gather in huge flocks, but during breeding this bird tends to remain in smaller colonies. It almost always nest in man-made structures such as bridges and barns, constructing nests out of mud pellets and plant fibers attached onto a vertical surface. It lays 3–6 white eggs with brown and gray spots which are incubated for 14–18 days. Young birds leave the nest after 3 weeks. It spends most of its time in the air, where it flies gracefully, feeding on a variety of winged insects.

SIZE 6¾ inches

DESCRIPTION Slender body, long pointed wings, and long, deeply forked tail. Blue-black head and upperparts, buffy white underparts. Forehead and throat are chestnut red. White spots undertail

HABITAT Anywhere where there are plenty of insects such as close to cattle. Rural buildings

SIMILAR SPECIES Coloring and shape are distinctive

BLACK-CAPPED CHICKADEE
(PARUS ATRICAPILLUS)

SIZE 5¼ inches

DESCRIPTION A long-tailed, short-billed songbird with large head. Black cap and bib contrasts with white face. Upperparts are gray and underparts are creamy white with rusty colored flanks. Darker gray wings and tail are edged with white feathers

HABITAT Deciduous and mixed open woodland and forest edges. Suburban parks and back yards

SIMILAR SPECIES Carolina Chickadee is smaller with comparatively smaller bib. Mountain Chickadee has white eyebrow. Chestnut-backed Chickadee has browner coloring

As a frequent winter visitor to bird feeders, the Black-capped Chickadee is a familiar sight across North America. It is constantly active in search of food, foraging for insects, seeds, and berries. During the breeding season, these birds will move into woodland in order to build loose nests in available tree holes. The female lays 4–8 white eggs with brown spots which are incubated for 10–12 days. The young leave the nest 2 weeks later. Juvenile birds closely resemble the adult. It has a sophisticated variety of calls, many of which are used to convey information to other birds in the flock.

BUSHTIT
(PSALTRIPARUS MINIMUS)

Commonly seen in flocks, these gregarious birds only leave the social group in order to breed and many will return to the same flock afterward. Flocks can be observed foraging for insects, moving rapidly through the trees maintaining contact with constant twittering and calling. Breeding pairs build tightly woven, gourd-shaped nests which are suspended from trees and hold between 5 and 14 white eggs. Both parents incubate the eggs, which hatch after 11–13 days and the young leave the nest 2 weeks later. Young Bushtits remain within the family group.

SIZE 4½ inches

DESCRIPTION Small songbird, with a long tail and a short bill. Plumage is gray, darker above and lighter beneath. Birds on the Pacific coast can have browner crowns, whilst some found near to Mexico have black cheeks

HABITAT Deciduous and mixed open woodland and forest edges. Some suburban parks and yards, particularly those with birdbaths

SIMILAR SPECIES Tail, bill and dull plumage make it distinctive. Although juvenile Verdins are similar they are never seen in flocks and they have a much shorter tail

TUFTED TITMOUSE
(PARUS BICOLOR)

The Tufted Titmouse is a sociable bird and can often be seen during winter in mixed flocks containing other chickadees, nuthatches, creepers, and woodpeckers. It also frequents bird feeders where it can dominate other smaller birds. Often observed clinging upside down on trees foraging for insects in bark, the Tufted Titmouse is an active and conspicuously noisy bird. It nests in tree cavities, laying 5–8 white and brown speckled eggs which the female incubates for 2 weeks. Fledglings leave the nest after 17–19 days. Although it prefers insects, it will eat fruit and seeds, especially sunflower seeds.

SIZE 6½ inches

DESCRIPTION A stocky songbird with a distinctive gray crest. Gray upperparts with pale gray below and buffy flanks. Its forehead is black, although in southern Texas birds have black crest and pale forehead

HABITAT Deciduous and mixed dense woodland, mature parks, and orchards

SIMILAR SPECIES Crest and coloring distinctive

RED-BREASTED NUTHATCH
(SITTA CANADENSIS)

This fairly common bird is often observed searching for food in pine trees, moving with agility around the outer branches and up and down trunks. It prefers the seeds from mature cones and will often horde excess food in larders for leaner times. During winter, the Red-breasted Nuthatch migrates south when food is particularly scarce. Breeding pairs will excavate a tree cavity, which is lined with feathers and moss. Five to eight white eggs with brown speckles are laid. These are incubated for 11–13 days then the chicks leave the nest between 19–22 days after hatching. Juvenile birds resemble the female. Nest cavities are often smeared with tree pitch around the entrance, probably in order to deter insects and other birds from entering the nest.

SIZE 4½ inches
DESCRIPTION Small and short-tailed bird with a straight gray bill. Black crown and black eye stripe, separated by a white eyebrow stripe. Its lower face and throat are white. The upperparts are blue gray and below it has a red breast, belly and underparts. The female is slightly paler and duller
HABITAT Conifer and mixed woodland
SIMILAR SPECIES Coloring makes it distinctive from other nuthatches

BROWN CREEPER (CERTHIA AMERICANA)

SIZE 5¼ inches

DESCRIPTION Small and slender with a small, curved bill and a long thin tail. Upperparts are brown with white spots, underparts are white with a rusty rump. Face has a white eyebrow

HABITAT Prefers coniferous forests, but can also be found anywhere with dead and decaying trees

SIMILAR SPECIES Creeping behavior make it unmistakable

Its mottled plumage provides excellent camouflage for the Brown Creeper as it spirals up tree trunks in search of insects and larvae. When foraging for food at the upper levels of the tree, it creeps along the underside of the branches. Birds in northern states and at higher altitudes will usually migrate southward during winter, often joining mixed flocks of nuthatches and chickadees in the forests to the south of North America. During the breeding season, the Brown Creeper builds a nest of bark and twigs bound with spiderweb, concealed behind the loose bark of a conifer. It lays 4–8 white eggs speckled with brown and incubates them for 2 weeks. Fledglings leave the nest 2 weeks after hatching.

(TROGLODYTES AEDON) HOUSE WREN

The House Wren is fiercely territorial and will aggressively defend nest sites, even destroying the eggs of other competing species in the near vicinity. It will adopt a variety of sites for nest building, from man-made structures to natural cavities and holes. Twig nests lined with feathers contain 5–7 white eggs, with fine brown speckles and these are incubated for 2 weeks by the female. The young leave the nest 2–3 weeks after hatching. It feeds mainly on insects and spiders. The House Wren is common across the continent, it is often seen and heard in suburban yards, visiting feeders and singing its loud, musical song.

SIZE 4¾ inches
DESCRIPTION Small and slender with a long slightly curved bill and short tail. Upperparts are gray-brown, with delicate black barring on wings and tail. Eastern birds are browner above. Underparts are pale gray and buffy, with dark bars on belly and undertail. Faint eyebrow and eyering
HABITAT Establishes territories in scrubland, agricultural land, forest edges, and open woodland and some suburban areas
SIMILAR SPECIES Winter Wren is smaller with more prominent barring on belly and flanks

WINTER WREN (TROGLODYTES TROGLODYTES)

SIZE 4 inches

DESCRIPTION Small and slender, with a short, often upright tail and a short, thin bill. Upperparts are reddish-brown and breast is buffy. Belly and undertail have prominent dark bars, wings are also barred with black. Faint eyebrow stripe

HABITAT Prefers cooler coniferous forests and wet woodland. Dense woodland with deeply shaded forest floors covered in dead wood and moss

SIMILAR SPECIES House Wren is larger with less prominent barring on belly and flanks

The tiny brown Winter Wren is difficult to spot as it rushes along the forest floor in search of the insects on which it mainly feeds. Although it often flits from tree to tree in flight, it tends to remain near the forest floor, building its nests in the roots of an upturned tree on or near the ground. It lays 4–7 white eggs, finely speckled with brown, which are incubated for 14–16 days by the female. Fledglings leave the nest 2–3 weeks after hatching. Birds further north or at higher altitude will migrate toward the southeastern United States for winter and return in early spring.

(CINCLUS MEXICANUS) AMERICAN DIPPER

The American Dipper can be found alongside fast-flowing, clear, rocky streams where it feeds from the gravelly floor. It will either walk through the shallows, dipping its head into the water, or dive into deeper water, rushing along the stream floor with wings slightly outstretched. It eats aquatic insects and water snails. Nests are always constructed near to water, on a ledge, in a crevice or roots, or under a bridge. Bulky constructions of grass and moss contain 3–6 white eggs which are incubated by the female for over 2 weeks. Young leave the nest 21–25 days after hatching.

SIZE 7½ inches

DESCRIPTION Large and stocky, with a slender bill and long, pale legs. It has slate-gray plumage throughout, with a slightly browner head. White eyelids can be seen when it blinks

HABITAT Found near fast-flowing mountain streams

SIMILAR SPECIES Behavior and habitat make it unique

BLUE-GRAY GNATCATCHER
(POLIOPTILA CAERULEA)

SIZE 4¼ inches

DESCRIPTION Small body, pointed wings, long tail, and long pale bill. Upperparts are blue-gray, underparts are white. Tail is black edged with white feathers and it has white secondary wing feathers. Narrow white eye ring. Female paler gray than male

HABITAT Prefers moist, deciduous woodland, but can be found in scrub, swamps, and desert

SIMILAR SPECIES Size and tail length are distinctive. The Black-tailed Gnatcatcher has darker tail when seen from below

The Blue-gray Gnatcatcher feeds at the tips of branches, flicking its long tail from side to side in order to scare out its insect prey. Toward the east, it can be found living high in leafy trees, but further west it will venture lower in the canopy. It breeds in a variety of habitats, from woodland to scrubland, often close to water for the abundance of food. Breeding males are flushed with blue with a black eyebrow. Tiny nests woven out of grass and plant fibers are hidden on tree branches and contain 4–5 pale blue eggs, sometimes spotted with brown. These are incubated for 2 weeks by both parents and the young leave the nest 9–12 days after hatching. Young birds resemble the female.

RUBY-CROWNED KINGLET
(REGULUS CALENDULA)

A tiny bird, the Ruby-crowned Kinglet is almost constantly in motion, flicking its wings. It is rarely seen since in summer it forages high up in the tree canopy. It builds its nest high in the trees, constructing a tightly woven open cup out of grasses, needles, bark, and feathers suspended from a branch. For such a small bird it lays a large clutch of between 5 and 12 creamy white eggs with brown and gray speckles. These are incubated for 2 weeks and the young leave the nest 2 weeks later. Young birds resemble the adults. It feeds mainly on insects but will eat fruit.

SIZE 4¼ inches

DESCRIPTION Small with a short, thin bill and slightly notched, short tail. Upperparts are olive, underparts are paler olive to buffy. White wing bars and an incomplete white eyering. Yellow edges to the flight feather and tail. Male has a red crown patch, not always visible

HABITAT Coniferous and mixed woodland, and thickets.

SIMILAR SPECIES Hutton's Vireo is similar but with a thicker bill. Golden-crowned Kinglet has a white eyebrow and bright yellow crown. Warblers are larger and lack the broken eyering

GOLDEN-CROWNED KINGLET
(REGULUS SATRAPA)

Although quite tame with humans, the Golden-crowned Kinglet is usually found at the top of conifer trees foraging for food, often hanging upside down from the tips of branches. It eats insects and larvae which it gathers from the tree's needles, hopping between branches and flicking its wings. Nesting birds are aggressively territorial and will display their crowns toward any rival or predator. Delicate nests of lichen, moss, and spiderweb are built suspended from high branches and contain 5–11 gray-white eggs spotted with brown and lilac. After an incubation period of 2 weeks, fledglings are ready to leave within 3 weeks of hatching.

SIZE 4 inches

DESCRIPTION Small with short tail and short, slim bill. Plumage is olive green above and buffy/white below, with white wing bars. Yellow crown surrounded by black, with a white eyebrow and a black eye stripe. Males have an orange patch in the center of the yellow crown

HABITAT Prefers dense coniferous woodland, but can be found in mixed forests

SIMILAR SPECIES Head coloring distinguishes it from the Ruby-crowned Kinglet

VARIED THRUSH
(IXOREUS NAEVIUS)

A shy and elusive songbird, the Varied Thrush will keep hidden in its tree habitat, either in the canopy or within the undergrowth, where its color and pattern act as camouflage. It builds large cup nests of twigs, leaves, and mud up in trees and lays 3–5 pale blue, brown-spotted eggs. These are incubated by the female for 2 weeks. Juvenile birds are paler, with a whitish belly and speckled underparts, and lack the dark breastband. It forages for food on the forest floor, clearing areas in search of insects and spiders. It also feeds on fruit and seeds.

SIZE 9½ inches
DESCRIPTION A large thrush with a relatively long neck and short tail. Crown, back, face, and breast band are gray-black. Throat, chest, and eyebrow stripe are burnt orange, dark wings have orange wing stripes seen in flight, which are partially revealed when at rest. Buffy-white belly. Females are duller than males
HABITAT Breeds in wet coniferous and mixed forests. Prefers dense, mature woodland
SIMILAR SPECIES Plumage is distinctive

AMERICAN ROBIN
(TURDUS MIGRATORIUS)

Perhaps the best known and most easily recognized American bird, the American Robin is common in suburban yards across the continent. It eats both fruit and insects, but can often be seen foraging on grass in search of earthworms. Large numbers of this bird tend to roost together, and during summer the roosts consist mainly of male birds since the females will sleep on the nest. It builds its nest in a shrub, tree or building, constructing a sturdy open cup of sticks, roots, grass and mud lined with moss. Three to four blue eggs are laid and incubated by the female and the young leave the nest 2–3 weeks after hatching. Juvenile birds lack the red breast and are spotted beneath.

SIZE 10 inches

DESCRIPTION Large and sturdy, with long legs and tail, a thin yellow bill. Upperparts are gray-brown, throat is streaked with white, breast and belly are red-orange. Undertail is white, and a broken white eye ring. Female is slightly paler than the male

HABITAT Forests, woodlands, swamps, and suburban parks and gardens containing grass, shrubs, and trees

SIMILAR SPECIES Plumage is distinctive

HERMIT THRUSH (CATHARUS GUTTATUS)

SIZE 6¾ inches

DESCRIPTION A small, stocky thrush with short wings and a thin bill. Upperparts are olive-brown, underparts are white, with grayish flanks. Reddish tail. Dark spotting on the throat and breast. White eye ring and pink legs

HABITAT Coniferous and mixed woodland

SIMILAR SPECIES Very similar to other *catharus* thrushes. Rusty rump provides some distinction, whilst Gray-cheeked and Bicknell's Thrushes lack eye ring. Veeries have less spotting on the breast

Although difficult to distinguish from other thrushes, the Hermit Thrush can be identified through its behavior and song. It has a habit of flicking its tail and wings, often on the point of landing, when it quickly raises then slowly lowers its tail. Its song is loud and slow, moving up and down the scale and repeating phrases. Its call is a soft *chup*. Although common, it spends much time hidden in the undergrowth foraging for food. Nests are built low, often on or just above the ground. Cups of grass and leaves are lined with moss and contain 3–5 blue-green eggs. These are incubated by the female for 12–14 days and young birds leave the nest 10–12 days after hatching.

(SIALIA CURRUCOIDES) MOUNTAIN BLUEBIRD

The Mountain Bluebird's preferred habitat is high open country, but it does need trees nearby for cover and nesting sites. It can often be found inhabiting recently burned woodland where there are plenty of dead trees with abandoned Woodpecker nest cavities. Once it has lined the bottom of its chosen cavity with bark, chippings, and feathers, it lays 4–6 pale blue-green eggs which are incubated for 2 weeks. Mountain Bluebirds can cope with low temperatures, but loose flocks often migrate to lower elevations during particularly harsh winters. It eats mainly insects and spiders, swooping upon its prey. During winter it relies on berries.

SIZE 7¼ inches

DESCRIPTION Long tail, long wings, and a thin bill. Males are bright blue, with underparts lighter than upperparts and no brown coloring. Females have duller blue wing and tail, with the remainder of the plumage being brown-gray. She also has a whitish rump and an eye ring

HABITAT Prefers high, open country such as mountain meadows

SIMILAR SPECIES Indigo Bunting is darker blue than the male. Female has longer wings and tail than other bluebirds

EASTERN BLUEBIRD
(SIALIA SIALIS)

Eastern Bluebirds favor tree cavities and hollows for nesting sites and the trend for clearing out dead wood from forests has had a negative impact on their numbers, as has increased competition for sites from birds such as European Starlings. In some areas this decline has been reversed due to the establishment of special nesting boxes. It lines a nest cavity with grass and plant material and then lays 2–7 pale blue-white eggs, which the female incubates for 2 weeks. Young birds leave the nest 3 weeks later. The Eastern Bluebird feeds on insects and berries found on or close to the ground, often dropping down from its perch to catch the prey. It tends to migrate only during harsh winters when food is scarce.

Size 7 inches

Description Stocky, short tail, short wings and stout bill. Upperparts are bright blue, chestnut-red throat, breast and sides. Belly and undertail are white. Females are duller with gray crown and back and white eye ring

Habitat Open countryside, agricultural land, forest edges, and open woodland

Similar Species Western Bluebird has a blue throat and male Mountain Bluebird lacks chestnut coloring

GRAY CATBIRD
(DUMETELLA CAROLINENSIS)

SIZE 8½ inches

DESCRIPTION Slender body and long tail. Plumage slate-gray overall, with near black tail and black cap. Undertail is rufus red

HABITAT Prefers dense vegetation, such as woodland thickets and shrubs

SIMILAR SPECIES Coloring of plumage is distinctive

The Gray Catbird earns its name from its call which mimics that of a cat's *meow* although it is an accomplished mimic of other birds too. Its preference for dense shrubbery has enabled it to flourish in suburban areas and it will often be found, or heard, in parks and yards. It feeds primarily on insects, spiders, ants, and caterpillars, for which it forages on the ground but during summer and fall it relies far more on fruit and berries for its diet. It builds its well-concealed nest in a thick shrub, or low in a tree and lays 3–5 blue-green eggs. These are incubated by the female and hatch after 12–14 days. Young birds leave the nest 9–15 days later.

NORTHERN MOCKINGBIRD
(MIMUS POLYGLOTTOS)

A common bird in the Southern Hemisphere, the Northern Mockingbird is gradually expanding its range further north. It is well-known for its lengthy, complicated song which often includes the mimicked calls of other birds. Mockingbirds are excellent mimics and can copy noises not made by birds, including sounds such as sirens and machinery. Distinctive behavior includes occasionally flicking its tail from side to side and flashing its wings whilst foraging, possibly to scare out insects. Open cup nests made of twigs lined with grasses are hidden low in shrubs and trees and contain 3–5 blue-green eggs. These are incubated by the female and hatch after 12–13 days with young birds leaving the nest 9–12 days later. Its diet consists mainly of insects, spiders, and berries.

SIZE 10 inches

DESCRIPTION Slender body, long tail, short, slim bill. Upperparts are gray, underneath is white. At rest shows two white wing bars, in flight a large white wing patch. Black tail with white outer feathers

HABITAT Woodland, scrubland, desert, farmland, and urban areas

SIMILAR SPECIES Shrikes have black masks and thicker bills

BROWN THRASHER (TOXOSTOMA RUFUM)

SIZE 11½ inches

DESCRIPTION Large and stocky, with long pointed wings and long tail. Crown, nape and upperparts are red-brown. Underparts are white with heavy black streaks. Face is gray and eye is yellow. Two white wing bars and white corners to tail

HABITAT Prefers dense vegetation in hedgerows, thickets, forest edges, and brush

SIMILAR SPECIES Long-billed Thrasher has longer bill, orange eyes, and grayer plumage. Thrushes are spotted below with shorter tails

Fairly common to the southeast, the Brown Thrasher is usually only observed when it is in full song during the breeding season, the rest of the time remaining concealed within its habitat. It has one of the largest song repertoires in North America. It feeds mainly on insects, spiders, and berries, foraging on the ground with its bill. It is an aggressive defender of its twig cup nest, which is well hidden on the ground or in dense brush. The female lays 2–4 bluish-white eggs with brown speckles and these are incubated by both parents for 2 weeks. Young birds leave the nest 2 weeks after hatching.

(STURNUS VULGARIS) EUROPEAN STARLING

A small number of European Starlings were introduced to New York in 1890 as part of a project to bring to North America all the birds mentioned in the works of Shakespeare. Today, the European Starling is the most abundant bird in North America. Its ability to exploit man-made environments and to feed from a wide variety of food sources has contributed to its incredible population increase. It competes with other birds, often displacing them from their nests in order to lay its own clutch of 5–6 pale blue eggs. These are incubated by both parents for 2 weeks and the young leave the nest 3 weeks after hatching. Juvenile birds are gray-brown with pale underparts. It can often be seen in large flocks performing aerobatic displays.

SIZE 8½ inches

DESCRIPTION Plump body, short tail, and long, pointed bill. Plumage is almost black, during summer shows a purple and green sheen with upperparts marked with brown spots and underparts plain. During fall and winter plumage is duller and heavily spotted with white all over. Bill is yellow most of the time, becoming darker during fall

HABITAT Prefers open countryside and agricultural land, common in urban areas such as parks, yards, and garbage tips

SIMILAR SPECIES Its size, coloring, and habitat are all distinctive

CEDAR WAXWING
(BOMBYCILLA CEDRORUM)

The Cedar Waxwing specializes in eating fruit and can survive on nothing else for months. Its preference for fruit and berries dictates much of its behavior and large flocks will move about in search of feeding grounds, particularly in winter. Although it is frugivorous it will also eat flying insects which it catches in flight. It tends to breed late in the year and lays 3–6 blue-gray eggs in a loose nest of twigs and grasses woven onto a tree branch. After being incubated for 12–14 days the young leave the nest 17–19 days after hatching. Juvenile birds are similar to adults but streaky below.

Size 7¼ inches
Description Rounded body, short tail, short, thin bill and crested head. Upperparts are pale brown fading to darker, gray-brown on back. Underparts are buffy-yellow with white under tail. Dark wings have yellow and white markings and a red spot. Black face mask is edged with white, black chin. Yellow tip on tail
Habitat Breeds in open woodland and riparian areas. Winters in areas where there are fruit bearing trees
Similar Species Bohemian Waxwing is larger with grayer belly and red under tail

BOHEMIAN WAXWING (BOMBYCILLA GARRULUS)

SIZE 8¼ inches

DESCRIPTION Stocky and plump, short tail, short bill, and crested head. Pale brown head and crest fades into cinnamon-gray upperparts and plain gray underparts. Darker gray wings have yellow-white wing markings and a red spot, dark tail has yellow tip. Black eye mask edged with white and black chin. Undertail feathers are chestnut brown

HABITAT Pine and spruce forests, open coniferous and mixed woodland, parks, and gardens

SIMILAR SPECIES Cedar Waxwing is smaller, browner and lacks chestnut under tail

Its preference for fruit means that the Bohemian Waxwing is non-territorial and flocks will move far in search of feeding grounds. Although it tends to remain in the far north during the winter, it is a regular visitor to the states and provinces along the North America/Canada border and will venture further southward to the west. During breeding it builds an open twig nest lined with moss high in a conifer tree. It lays 4–6 bluish eggs which are incubated for 12–14 days and the hatchlings leave the nest 2 weeks later. Juvenile birds are similar but streaky below. Its diet consists mainly of fleshy fruits and berries and insects.

(DENDROICA PETECHIA) YELLOW WARBLER

The Yellow Warbler is a widespread bird which breeds as far north as Alaska and as far south as Georgia and South Carolina. It migrates during the winter, heading for Central America, but some only fly to Mexico. It eats mainly insects and spiders, for which it forages in the foliage of trees. It builds its cup nest in the crotch of a small tree out of twigs lined with down. The nest is often parasitized by the Cowbird who will leave its egg in that of the Yellow Warbler, who responds by building another nest on top of the original. Nests have been found with several tiers as a result of this behavior. The Yellow Warbler itself lays 4–5 white eggs with brown spots and incubates these for 9–10 days. Young birds leave the nest 10–12 days after hatching.

SIZE 5 inches

DESCRIPTION Stout body, short tail, thick bill. Yellow plumage, wings and tail are yellow-olive with yellow feather edges. Male has chestnut streaks on breast and flanks. Dark eye

HABITAT Prefers wet deciduous woodland for breeding, including willows and alders. Further south found in mangroves

SIMILAR SPECIES Wilson's and Hooded Warblers have dark caps. Duller females difficult to tell apart

BLACKBURNIAN WARBLER
(DENDROICA FUSCA)

SIZE 5 inches

DESCRIPTION Slender, long tailed, pointed wings. Breeding male has black crown and eye stripe, orange eyebrow, throat and ear patch, black back with white stripes and black wing with white patch. Fine black streaks on white flanks. Orange breast becomes white under belly and undertail. Female similar but with a more yellow throat and white wing bars

HABITAT Coniferous and mixed forests

SIMILAR SPECIES Unmistakable

Although confined to the conifererous forests of the northeast, the Blackburnian Warbler is common within its range. During fall it joins mixed flocks to migrate southward to South America and its coloring can mean it is easily spotted. In its breeding habitat it tends to remain high up in the branches of the trees where it forages for food and in this way does not compete with other warblers. It nests up high also, and builds a large cup of twigs, leaves and vegetable matter which holds 4–5 greenish-white eggs. These are incubated for 10–12 days by the female. The Blackburnian Warbler feeds mainly on insects and berries.

YELLOW-RUMPED WARBLER
(DENDROICA CORONATA)

Previously known as the Myrtle Warbler in the east and Audubon's Warbler in the west, these two species overlapped and are now considered one species; the Yellow-rumped Warbler. During the summer it can be found across the north of the continent and in fall it migrates southward to Central America. However, its ability to consume bayberries and wax myrtle means it can winter further north than other warblers. It eats insects and spiders as well as berries and fruit. During breeding it nests high in conifers, building twig cups on horizontal branches. It lays 4–5 white eggs with brown and gray spots, which are incubated for 12–13 days. Hatchlings leave the nest after 10–12 days.

SIZE 5½ inches

DESCRIPTION Long tail and relatively stout bill. Upperparts are dark gray with black streaks. Whitish underparts with black streaks on flanks, white tail spots. Breeding male has bright yellow rump and yellow patch on each flank and a yellow crown. Audubon's form has yellow throat and white wing patch; Myrtle form has white eyebrow and white throat with two white wing bars

HABITAT Coniferous and mixed woodland, parks, and gardens

SIMILAR SPECIES Relatively distinctive, but the variation in coloring as a result of combining two different species can lead to some confusion

MAGNOLIA WARBLER
(DENDROICA MAGNOLIA)

A common and more conspicuous warbler, the Magnolia Warbler summers in the north and can be seen across the east as it begins its migration during fall. Its name derives from its discovery in 1810 in a Mississippian Magnolia tree but this is the only connection. It tends to prefer conifer trees for nest building, when it builds a loose shallow cup of grasses and roots on a low horizontal branch. The female lays 3–5 creamy white eggs which she then incubates for 2 weeks. Young birds leave the nest 9 days after hatching. Juvenile birds resemble non-breeding adults. Its diet consists mainly of insects and spiders, for which it forages on the underside of conifer needles and deciduous foliage.

SIZE 5 inches

DESCRIPTION Small with round head, small bill and long tail. Male has dark gray upperparts with white edging on wing feathers. Underparts are bright yellow with black streaks on breast and rump. Crown is pale gray, white eyebrow streak and black face mask. Females and non breeding males are olive gray above, lack the face mask, have a white eye-ring and have a faint gray breast band

HABITAT Prefers small conifers such as young spruce. Damp and open coniferous and mixed woodland

SIMILAR SPECIES Juvenile Prairie Warbler similar to juvenile Magnolia Warbler, but lacks white eye ring

BLACK-AND-WHITE WARBLER
(MNIOTILTA VARIA)

SIZE 5¼ inches

DESCRIPTION Small, short tail and long, slender decurved bill. Plumage is mainly black with white streaks. Prominent white eyebrow stripe and white wing bars. Breeding males have black throat and cheeks, non-breeding males show a white throat. Females have buffy flanks with gray streaks

HABITAT Mature deciduous and mixed forests

SIMILAR SPECIES Breeding male Blackpoll Warbler has black cap, Black-throated Gray Warbler has black crown

The Black-and-white Warbler has both distinctive plumage and behavior. It creeps about on the lower branches and trunks of trees foraging for insect food. It has particularly long hind toes and claws to enable it to cling to the bark and it uses its long bill to root out insects and spiders. It builds its open cup nest of leaves and grasses on the ground next to a tree and lays 4–5 creamy-whitish eggs with brown speckles. These are incubated for 9–12 days and the young leave the nest 1–2 weeks after hatching. Juvenile birds resemble the female. The Black-and-white Warbler is a particularly aggressive defender of its territory and will regularly attack other bird species.

COMMON YELLOWTHROAT

(GEOTHLYPIS TRICHAS)

The common and distinctive Yellowthroat spends much of its time hidden in dense undergrowth, usually in a marshy area. During the breeding season the male can be seen performing aerial displays before dropping to the ground, or perching on a high stalk singing its high-pitched song. It nests in the undergrowth, concealing a bulky woven cup of grasses among weeds and growing grass. It often takes a complicated route to arrive at the nest in order to confuse possible predators. The female lays 3–6 white eggs with brown splotches which are incubated for 11–12 days and the young are ready to leave a week after hatching. Its diet consists mainly of insects which it gleans from the undergrowth.

SIZE 5 inches

DESCRIPTION Small and stocky with short neck, small bill, rounded tail and wings. Male's upperparts are olive-green, below has bright yellow throat and breast fading to white belly and brownish flanks. Black face mask with white upperborder. Female brownish-olive above and duller yellow below fading to buffy white. Broken white eye ring

HABITAT Prefers thick vegetation in a range of areas, although usually close to water

SIMILAR SPECIES Adult male very distinctive. Females and juveniles are similar to Mourning Warbler, but this has yellow belly and olive breast band

AMERICAN REDSTART
(SETOPHAGA RUTICILLA)

The American Redstart uses its bold plumage to flush out insect prey from the foliage, flashing its wing and tail patches. Its diet consists mainly of insects and spiders, which are often caught in flight. This bird nests high above the ground, building a tightly woven cup nest out of grasses, bark, hair, and twigs held together with spider web. It lays 3–5 creamy-white eggs with dark speckles on the large end and these are incubated for 11–12 days. The young leave the nest 3 weeks after hatching. A common and distinctive member of the warbler family, the American Redstart can be seen across the north and southeast of North America during the summer before it migrates south toward Mexico and Central America in the fall.

SIZE 5¼ inches

DESCRIPTION Small body, long tail, rounded wings and short broad bill. Male has mainly black plumage, with bright orange patches on side of breast, wing, and tail feathers. Belly and undertail white. Female has gray upperparts with white below, yellow patches on side, wing, and outer tail feathers

HABITAT Moist, second-growth deciduous forests

SIMILAR SPECIES Coloring is distinctive

SCARLET TANAGER
(PIRANGA OLIVACEA)

Common to the eastern forest interior, the striking Scarlet Tanager is rarely seen because of its tendency to remain high in the forest canopy. It can be observed throughout the southeastern states during fall when it begins its migration south to the tropics for winter. It builds a shallow cup nest of grass and leaves high in a tree on a horizontal branch and this hold 3–5 blue-green eggs with delicate brown spots. These are incubated by the female for 2 weeks and the young leave the nest 10–12 days after hatching. Juvenile birds resemble the female. Its diet consists of insects, spiders, and berries, for which it will either forage in the canopy, or during colder weather, seek from the ground. As a result migrating birds are more often seen at ground level.

Size 7 inches

Description Medium sized with a stout, pointed bill. Male has brilliant red plumage with shiny black wings and tail during summer and greenish-yellow plumage replacing the scarlet out of breeding season. Female has olive back, yellow underparts and gray wings and tail with green outer feathers

Habitat Prefers mature deciduous and mixed woodland for breeding. Occasionally suburban areas with plenty of trees

Similar Species Male is distinctive. Female similar to Summer Tanager, but has gray tail instead of green

EASTERN TOWHEE (PIPILO ERYTHROPHTHALMUS)

Size 7½ inches
Description Stocky body, long tail, and rounded wings. Upperparts, head, and throat are black, red sides and flanks, white belly and undertail. Black wings have white wing patches and black tail has white outer feathers. Female is duller brown-black
Habitat Dense forest undergrowth and thickets. Prefers second-growth woodland
Similar Species Spotted Towhee has white spotting on wings, back, and tail corners

The Eastern Towhee is one half of what was once a single species, the Rufus-sided Towhee, now accepted as two separate species: the Eastern and the Spotted. In areas where the two overlap they will interbreed, but the Eastern Towhee, as its name suggests, is more commonly found in the southeast, whereas the Spotted Towhee is common to the west. Its diet consists mainly of insects, spiders, berries, and seeds for which it forages on the ground. Its foraging technique involves vigorously scratching at the ground with both feet in order to uncover its food. It builds nests on the ground out of grass, twigs and roots, laying 2–6 creamy green eggs spotted with brown. These are incubated by the female for 2 weeks and the young leave the nest 10–12 days after hatching.

(SPIZELLA PASSERINA) CHIPPING SPARROW

A common and widespread bird, the Chipping Sparrow can often be seen in suburban parks and yards where its trilling song is familiar. It will often feed out in the open, foraging on the ground and will visit bird feeders. During winter, many birds will remain in the same areas, although those further north may head south in large flocks. It builds a relatively flimsy nest of grass and plant fibers lined with hair in the branches of a tree or bush. These contain 3–5 pale blue eggs with brown, black and purple spots at the round end. The eggs are incubated by the female for up to 2 weeks, and the young leave the nest 9–12 days after hatching. It feeds mainly on small seeds and small fruit, grass, and insects.

SIZE 5½ inches

DESCRIPTION Medium-sized sparrow, long, slim, forked tail, dark conical bill. Rusty crown, white eyebrow stripe, black eye line. Face, collar, and underparts are pale gray. Back and wings are brown with dark streaks, wings show two white wing bars

HABITAT Open grassy woodland, grassy fields and forest edges

SIMILAR SPECIES Similar to other sparrows with rusty crowns. Field Sparrow has pink bill and white eye ring. Swamp Sparrow has rusty wings. American Tree Sparrow has dark breast spot. Winter plumage resembles Clay-colored and Brewer's Sparrows, but with gray rump rather than brown

AMERICAN TREE SPARROW
(SPIZELLA ARBOREA)

SIZE 6½ inches

DESCRIPTION Medium-sized sparrow, long, slim, forked tail, dark conical bill with yellow lower mandible. Rusty crown and eye stripe, gray face and neck. Upperparts are brown with dark streaks and two white wing bars. Underparts are gray, with black breast spot and rusty patches at the side

HABITAT Prefers open scrubby areas near trees for breeding. Winters in fields, suburban gardens, marshes, and open woodland

SIMILAR SPECIES Chipping and Field Sparrows are smaller and lack the dark breast spot

Common across Canada and the northern United States, the American Tree Sparrow can withstand colder temperatures and will spend its summers in the tundra zone. Its ability to tolerate sub-zero temperatures is linked to its food intake and during the summer it will exclusively eat insects then switch to seeds and berries during fall. It nests on or near to the ground, building an open cup of mosses and grass lined with feathers. This contains 4–5 pale blue eggs with brown speckles, which are incubated by the female for just under 2 weeks. Young birds are ready to leave the nest 9–11 days after hatching. Juveniles are similar to the adult but with streaking on the crown, nape, and breast.

SAVANNAH SPARROW
(PASSERCULUS SANDWICHENSIS)

Found in a variety of open habitats across North America, the Savannah Sparrow is widespread and common. It has 16 subspecies and consequently varieties of coloring can appear: some birds are much darker and more heavily streaked whilst others are light brown or rufus. During fall it joins large flocks to migrate southward. In summer, it builds a cup nest on the ground out of grass and plant fibers which it conceals among vegetation. It lays 4–6 whitish eggs with brown and purple spots and these are incubated for 10–12 days by both parents. The young leave the nest 2 weeks after hatching. The Savannah Sparrow forages on the ground for insects and food, either alone or in small flocks and is particularly adept at running along the ground.

SIZE 5½ inches

DESCRIPTION Compact body, short, forked tail, conical bill and crested crown. Upperparts are brown with dark streaks. Pale brown to buffy breast heavily streaked with dark stripes, belly white. Thin white crown stripe and white or yellowish eyebrow stripe

HABITAT Open country, salt marshes, grassy beaches, and tundra

SIMILAR SPECIES Vesper Sparrow has white eye ring and lacks eyebrow and crown stripes

FOX SPARROW (PASSERELLA ILIACA)

SIZE 7 inches

DESCRIPTION Large, stocky sparrow with round head, conical bill with dark upper mandible and yellow lower. Coloring varies from east to west; Eastern Fox Sparrow is gray streaked with rufus above, Western Fox Sparrow has dark brown/gray plumage above. Both have triangular spots arranged in stripes below which merge on breast. Belly is white, rump and tail either red or gray/brown

HABITAT Coniferous and mixed woodland, undergrowth, and mountain chaparral

SIMILAR SPECIES Hermit Thrush has white eye ring and lacks heavy streaking below

One of the largest sparrows in North America, despite its common status the Fox Sparrow is more usually seen during the spring migration than during its summer breeding season. It remains within dense undergrowth and thickets, where it builds its nest of plant fibers either on or near the ground. This contains 4–5 pale green eggs with brown speckles which are incubated by the female for up to 2 weeks. The young are ready to leave the nest after 9–11 days and juveniles resemble the adult but are duller. Its diet consists of seeds and insects and it forages on the ground with a distinctively vigorous scratching technique.

(MELOSPIZA MELODIA) SONG SPARROW

The most widespread sparrow in North America, the Song Sparrow is often seen in suburban back yards, where, as its name suggests, it is a persistent singer. Birds in different areas can vary in color: those found in the southwest are paler, whilst those from the Pacific northwest are darker with heavy streaks. It spends much of its time on or near to the ground, foraging for seeds, berries, and insects by scratching with both feet. Nests are well concealed on the ground, built out of grass and plant fibers and contain 3–6 greenish-white eggs with brown spots. These are incubated for 2 weeks by the female and the young are independent some 10 days later. They tend to remain in a family group rather than join larger flocks.

SIZE 5½–7½ inches

DESCRIPTION Compact and stocky, round head, conical bill, long tail. Coloring can vary, generally brown back with red-brown streaks and brown-red streaked wings. Underparts white with heavy dark stripes and streaks, central black breast spot. Brown crown with gray face and eyebrow. Light gray crown stripe

HABITAT Open and shrubby areas, often near water. Thickets, parks, and gardens

SIMILAR SPECIES Lincoln's Sparrow is generally smaller, less streaked and more buffy below, without central breast spot. Savannah Sparrow lacks breast spot and has shorter tail

WHITE-CROWNED SPARROW
(ZONOTRICHIA LEUCOPHRYS)

SIZE 7 inches

DESCRIPTION Large and stocky, long tail, pink or yellow conical bill. Upperparts are gray-brown streaked, black and white striped crown, gray face and underparts. White throat and belly and two white wing bars

HABITAT Breeds in tundra, alpine meadows, and boreal forests. Also found in woodland edges, scrubland, and thickets

SIMILAR SPECIES White-throated Sparrow is browner with a dark bill. Golden-crowned Sparrow has yellow crown stripe and lacks white on the head

The White-crowned Sparrow is important to those who study bird behavior and migratory patterns. Males learn their songs within the first few months of life from their environment, and because they tend not to move from their territories, song dialects emerge. They are also influenced by daylight hours, and birds in the extreme north will often sing throughout the night. It weaves a grass nest high in a tree and lays 3–5 pale blue eggs with red-brown spots. The female incubates these for 12–17 days and the young are fledged 10–12 days later. They move in mixed flocks, usually with White-throated Sparrows. This bird's diet consists mainly of seeds, grains, and insects for which they forage on the ground.

WHITE-THROATED SPARROW
(ZONOTRICHIA ALBICOLLIS)

During the winter in the southeast of the continent, the White-throated Sparrow can often be seen in migratory flocks and will often visit urban parks and gardens. Flocks gather to roost during the evening on dense thickets and its call is a familiar sound. It feeds on seeds, berries, and insects, mostly gleaned from the ground. It breeds in the cooler north during summer, building a nest of moss, grass, and plant fibers on the ground. This contains 3–5 greenish-white eggs spotted with brown at the round end. The female incubates them for 2 weeks and the young birds leave the nest 10–12 days later. Juveniles are brown and buff with fine streaks on the breast.

SIZE 6¾ inches

DESCRIPTION Large, stocky, long slightly forked tail, dark conical bill. Chestnut brown above with dark streaks. Black and white head stripes, gray cheeks and breast, conspicuous white throat. White belly. Bright yellow spot behind bill, two white wing bars

HABITAT Coniferous and mixed woodland with dense undergrowth, scrubland, brush, and urban areas

SIMILAR SPECIES White-crowned Sparrow is grayer with pink or yellow bill

YELLOW-EYED JUNCO

(JUNCO PHAEONOTUS)

The Yellow-eyed Junco spends much of its time on the ground where it can be seen running or purposefully walking rather than hopping. The female lays 3–5 pale gray or bluish white eggs marked with reddish brown, in an open nest of dried grass lined with hair and built on the ground. Incubation takes 15 days and is carried out by the female, who produces two or three broods in a year. The young are ready to leave the nest 2 weeks later. Its diet consists mainly of seeds, berries, and insects. The Yellow-eyed Junco is common only in the far south of North America, particularly southeastern Arizona.

SIZE 6¼ inches

DESCRIPTION Slender body, long tail, conical bill with dark upper mandible and orange lower. Gray head, sides and flanks. Rust-red back and wings. Pale gray breast and whitish belly. Dark tail with white outer feathers. Yellow eye

HABITAT Resident in mountainous coniferous and pine/oak forests

SIMILAR SPECIES Dark-eyed Junco has dark eye, pink bill and hops

DARK-EYED JUNCO (JUNCO HYEMALIS)

SIZE 6¼ inches

DESCRIPTION Medium sized sparrow, slender body, long tail. Color can vary geographically, all are unstreaked gray or brown, with a gray to black hood, white belly and white outer tail feathers. Eyes dark, legs pink

HABITAT Breeds in coniferous and mixed forest. Winters in fields, agricultural land, scrub, and urban areas

SIMILAR SPECIES Outer tail feathers are unusual in other sparrows. Yellow-eyed Junco has yellow eyes, reddish, wings and walks rather than hops

The Dark-eyed Junco is a familiar winter visitor and is identified by its plain plumage, dark hood, and white outer tail feathers. Dark-eyed Juncos come in a number of color forms, five of which were once considered separate species. The "Oregon" is black/brown and found to the west. The "Slate-colored" is the grayest, found in the east, from Alaska to Texas. The "Gray-headed" has a brown back and gray sides and breeds in the Rockies; the "White-winged" from South Dakota is all gray with white wing bars and "Guadelupe" is from California and a dull brown. Two other forms, the "Pink-sided" with a gray hood and pink sides and the "Red-backed" which is gray with a red back are also distinguishable. All produce clutches of 3–5 blue-white eggs and all feed on insects, seeds, and berries.

(PLECTROPHENAX NIVALIS) SNOW BUNTING

The Snow Bunting is a common winter visitor from the Arctic north of the continent where it breeds further north than almost any other land bird. It is most commonly seen in its non-breeding plumage during migration periods, in large mixed flocks of foraging birds. It prefers barren, rocky ground for breeding, lining a ground crevice with moss and feathers to hold 4–6 blue-white eggs with brown and lilac spots. These are incubated by the female for 2 weeks, with the male defending the site. The young are ready to leave 11–18 days after hatching. It feeds mainly on insects, spiders, and weed and grass seeds for which it forages on the ground.

SIZE 6¾ inches
DESCRIPTION Chunky body, flat head, thick bill, forked tail, short wings. Breeding male has pure white body with black back, black wing tips and shoulder patch, and black central tail feathers. Winter male has buffy crown, collar, and back. Female has rusty crown, collar and back
HABITAT Open country, tundra, rocky shores, beaches, and barren fields
SIMILAR SPECIES Plumage distinctive

PAINTED BUNTING
(PASSERINA CIRIS)

Once a highly sought-after caged bird due to its spectacular coloring, the Painted Bunting is now under federal protection, although its conservation is still of concern. It is often referred to as the "Nonpareil" meaning without equal. Despite its bright plumage it is not easy to spot, since it hides and skulks in dense thickets and undergrowth. It is found mainly in the southeast of the continent during the breeding season, migrating further south into Central America for the winter. It nests close to the ground, building a cup of grass and plant fibers which holds 3–4 gray white eggs. These are incubated by the female for 11–13 days and the young leave the nest 2 weeks later. Its diet consists mainly of seeds, berries, and insects, gleaned from the ground.

SIZE 5½ inches
DESCRIPTION Small and stocky, short tail, rounded bill. Male has bright blue head, bright green back, blackish wings and tail, bright red underparts. Female has plain lime green upperparts and greenish-yellow underparts
HABITAT Woodland edges, dense thickets, and brush
SIMILAR SPECIES Coloring unmistakable

INDIGO BUNTING
(PASSERINA CYANEA)

The Indigo Bunting prefers abandoned land and cleared woodland and is rarely seen, despite being relatively common. Migrating birds move at night, using the stars for navigation, heading toward Central and South America. Although common to the east of North America, its range can overlap with that of the Lazuli Bunting in the west and the two will often interbreed. It feeds mainly on insects and seeds, for which it forages on the ground, usually in flocks. It builds a cup nest of grass and bark strips into the branches of a tree or bush and lays 3–5 pale blue-white eggs. The female incubates these for 11–14 days and the young leave the nest 9–11 days after hatching.

Size 5½ inches

Description Stocky body, short tail, small conical bill. Breeding male is deep indigo blue. Female and winter male have dark brown upperparts and paler brown underparts with fine streaks, faint wing bars and blue tint to tail

Habitat Prefers brushy pasture, open woodland, and forest edges and clearings. Also found in orchards, weedy agricultural land, and at roadside edges

Similar Species Male Blue Grosbeak is larger with bigger bill and wide brown wing bars. Eastern Bluebird has red chest and white belly

NORTHERN CARDINAL
(CARDINALIS CARDINALIS)

Common and popular, the Northern Cardinal lives in a variety of habitats and consequently is often seen in suburban parks and back yards. It mates for life and will return to the same breeding area each year and mated pairs communicate with complex songs. A nest is built above the ground with a loosely woven cup of twigs containing 3–4 pale green eggs with brown and lilac spots. The eggs are incubated by the female for 2 weeks, with the male providing food and assisting with the feeding. Hatchlings are ready to leave the nest 9–10 days later and the parents may produce a further 2 or 3 broods during the season. It feeds on the ground, in the open, foraging for insects, fruit, and seeds. Cardinals will also visit feeders for sunflower seeds.

SIZE 8¾ inches
DESCRIPTION Rounded body, long tail, large conical bill and crest. Male is bright red with slightly duller back and wings. Black face and chin and red bill. Female has red crest, wings, tail and bill, brown-gray upperparts and buffy underparts
HABITAT Forest edges, swamps, hedgerows, suburbs, and anywhere with small trees and shrubs
SIMILAR SPECIES Male unmistakable, female similar to Pyrrhuloxia, but this has a yellow decurved bill and grayer plumage

BLUE GROSBEAK
(GUIRACA CAERULEA)

Resident in the southern states of North America, the Blue Grosbeak migrates further south during fall. It will join small mixed flocks, consisting of other sparrows and finches, and can often be seen with them foraging for food, occasionally wagging its tail. It feeds mainly on seeds and insects, and its large bill enables it to consume larger types of both, including corn and grasshoppers. It nests in a low tree, building a loose cup of twigs and stems which holds 4–5 plain pale blue eggs. These are incubated by the female for 10–12 days and the young leave the nest 2 weeks after hatching. The female will then raise a second brood. Young birds resemble the female, although male juveniles will show a blue wash.

SIZE 6¾ inches

DESCRIPTION Stocky body, large head, large conical bill. Male has dark blue plumage with two broad cinnamon wing bars and black at base of silvery bill. Wings and tail appear almost black. Female is brown rather than blue with faint streaks

HABITAT Forest edges, fields, hedgerows, riversides, areas with medium-sized trees

SIMILAR SPECIES Indigo Bunting is smaller with smaller bill

RED-WINGED BLACKBIRD
(AGELAIUS PHOENICEUS)

Abundant across most of the North American continent, the Red-winged Blackbird can be found near to any body of water. It tends to gather in huge flocks, often containing other species of blackbird and only leaves the flock during the breeding season. It builds its nest close to the ground, weaving a cup of grass into reeds or a bush. This contains 3–5 pale blue-green eggs with brown and black spotes, which are incubated by the female for 10–12 days. Young birds leave the nest 2 weeks later and resemble the adult female. Pairs can raise 2 or 3 broods in a season and males may also take several mates. It feeds on grain during the spring, which results in its being considered a pest; however, it also eats crop-damaging insects.

SIZE 8¾ inches
DESCRIPTION Stocky body, long tail and rounded wings. Male is predominantly black with bright red shoulder patch, occasionally edged with yellow. Female is streaked brown with buff eyebrow
HABITAT Freshwater marshes, grassland, meadows, and open fields
SIMILAR SPECIES Male Tricolored Blackbird has red and white shoulder patch

BOBOLINK (DOLICHONYX ORYZIVORUS)

Size 7 inches

Description Slender body, pointed tail, pointed wings, short conical bill. Male is mostly black, buffy-yellow nape, white shoulder patches and rump. Female and winter male are buffy with dark streaks on back, rump and sides, dark wing and tail with pale edging and buff and black head stripes

Habitat Prefers open grassland and fields for breeding. During migration will use marshland and damp meadows

Similar Species Male is distinctive. Female Red-winged Blackbird is darker with longer bill

Like other blackbird species the male Bobolink performs elaborate courtship displays and uses its distinctive coloring to make it stand out, helping him to take several mates in a season. After breeding, the Bobolink reverts to its camouflage plumage and joins large mixed flocks to migrate to the Southern Hemisphere for winter. A breeding pair builds a flimsy grass cup nests on the ground, well concealed in dense vegetation. The female lays 4–7 pale gray eggs with lilac and brown blotches, which she incubates for 2 weeks. The young leave the nest 2 weeks after hatching. It forages on the ground for seeds, grain, insects, and spiders.

(STURNELLA MAGNA) EASTERN MEADOWLARK

A member of the blackbird family rather than the lark family, the Eastern Meadowlark is familiar on the open grasslands of the southeastern corner of North America. It can overlap in range with its relative the Western Meadowlark and the two will interbreed. Its song is a series of clear whistles, and its call a buzz and chatter. A breeding pair nests on the ground, building a grass cup with a domed roof. This contains 3–7 white eggs spotted with brown which are incubated by the female for 2 weeks. Young birds leave the nest 10–12 days after hatching. It feeds on insects, spiders, grass, and seeds for which it forages and probes the ground.

SIZE 9½ inches

DESCRIPTION Stocky body, short tail, long bill. Upperparts are brown with black streaks and bars, crown is black with buffy stripes. Gray cheeks, yellow throat, breast and belly with black breast band. White flanks and outer tail feathers

HABITAT Grassland, pastures, open countryside, golf courses

SIMILAR SPECIES Western Meadowlark almost identical, but slightly slimmer, best separated by voice

WESTERN MEADOWLARK
(STURNELLA NEGLECTA)

SIZE 9½ inches

DESCRIPTION Stocky body, short tail, long bill. Upperparts are brown with black streaks and bars, crown is black with buffy stripes. Gray cheeks, yellow throat, breast and belly with black breast band. White flanks and outer tail feathers

HABITAT Open countryside, grasslands, roadside and desert grassland

SIMILAR SPECIES Eastern Meadowlark almost identical, but slightly stockier, best separated by voice

An abundant and familiar bird across the western and south central states of the continent. The Western Meadowlark is closely related to the Eastern Meadowlark and where their range overlaps the two can be difficult to distinguish. The Western Meadowlark has a fluty whistling song and a sharp *chook chook* call. It feeds on insects, spiders, grass, and seeds for which it forages and probes the ground. During the breeding season, the male will take two mates at the same time, leaving the females to build the nests and rear the young. The nests are built of grass with a domed roof and concealed on the ground and hold 3–7 white eggs spotted with brown which are incubated for 2 weeks. Young birds leave the nest 10–12 days after hatching.

BREWER'S BLACKBIRD
(EUPHAGUS CYANOCEPHALUS)

The Brewer's Blackbird's preference for human-modified environments has enabled it to gradually spread its range westward across the continent and it is a common and familiar visitor to suburban and urban areas. It is a gregarious and sociable bird, nesting and gathering in large flocks which often contain other blackbirds and the Brown-headed Cowbird. It builds its bulky nest of twigs, grass and mud on the ground, often close to water. This contains 4–6 light gray eggs with brown and gray blotches and these are incubated by the female for 2 weeks. Young birds leave the nest 2 weeks after hatching and juveniles resemble the female. Its diet consists mainly of seeds, grain, and insects.

SIZE 9 inches

DESCRIPTION Slender body, long tail, straight pointed bill and yellow eye. Male has glossy black plumage with purple sheen to head and greenish-violet sheen on body. Female is gray-brown with a dark eye

HABITAT Prefers open, human-modified areas such as agricultural land, fields, urban parks, and grassy lawns

SIMILAR SPECIES Rusty Blackbird has longer, thinner bill and duller plumage

BROWN-HEADED COWBIRD
(MOLOTHRUS ATER)

Size 7½ inches
Description Slender, short tail, pointed wings, short conical bill, dark eye. Male has black plumage with brown sheen to head and green sheen to body. Female is light gray-brown with pale throat and pale streaks to underparts
Habitat Open country, farmland with grazing cattle, suburban areas
Similar Species Bronzed Cowbird has red eyes and larger body and bill

The Brown-headed Cowbird earns its name from its habit of feeding near to livestock, following in the wake of cattle to pick up insects kicked up by moving herds. Before humans enclosed cattle, pre-colonial Cowbirds would follow herds of bison across vast distances. As a result they took to depositing their eggs in the nests of other birds, and single eggs of white with brown speckles are often placed in the nest of finches, warblers, or vireos. The host parent incubates the cowbird egg, which then hatches to dominate the host nestlings. In this way, the growing numbers of Cowbirds are often accused of endangering the numbers of other birds. The Brown-headed Cowbird will often flock with other blackbirds outside the breeding season. It eats grain, seeds, berries, and insects.

COMMON GRACKLE
(QUISCALUS QUISCULA)

The gregarious and noisy Common Grackle is often seen traveling in huge flocks with other blackbirds and is a familiar sight in suburban gardens. It is an opportunistic feeder and will eat almost anything, from grain and insects to fish, eggs, fledgling birds, and mice. It will wade into water, visit feeders, and follow agricultural vehicles in its search for food. The clearing of forests and spread of human-modified environments has enabled it to extend its range and increase in numbers. Breeding grackles build bulky twig nests high in trees and lay 4–6 green eggs marked with brown. These are incubated by the female for 2 weeks and the young leave the nest 3 weeks after hatching. Juvenile birds are dark brown with brown eyes.

SIZE 12½ inches

DESCRIPTION Medium-sized, very long tail, long bill, yellow-white eyes. Male has black plumage with bronze sheen to body and blue sheen to head, purple gloss on tail. Female is smaller and duller

HABITAT Open areas with scattered trees, open woodland, swamps, marshes, and urban areas

SIMILAR SPECIES Long tail marks it out from other blackbirds

EVENING GROSBEAK
(COCCOTHRAUSTES VESPERTINUS)

Its distinctive coloring and bill make the
Evening Grosbeak a noticeable winter
visitor to bird feeders. It often gathers in
large, noisy flocks which can clean out
feeders in a very short amount of time. It
forages for food high in trees, eating
insects, seeds, buds, and fruit and its large
beak enables it to crack larger seeds. It
will breed in woodland, building loose
bowl nests of twigs and plant fibers in the
high branches of conifer trees. These hold
3–4 blue-green eggs with fine markings
which are incubated by the female for 2
weeks. Young birds leave the nest 2 weeks
after hatching and juveniles resemble the
female with gray-gold plumage.

SIZE 8 inches

DESCRIPTION Medium-sized, short tail, short pointed
wings, very large pale conical bill. Male has olive-
brown head, neck and upper back, black wings
with large white patches. Yellow forehead and
eyebrow, yellow underparts. Female has gray
upperparts with black wings and tail with white
wing patches

HABITAT Breeds in coniferous forests, winters
in coniferous or mixed forests and suburban
back yards

SIMILAR SPECIES Goldfinches are smaller with
smaller bill

RED CROSSBILL
(LOXIA CURVIROSTRA)

The Red Crossbill is dependent upon pine seeds and its shaped bill is designed to enable it to extract these from the cones. It moves in flocks through pine forests in search of food and is able to breed during any season, even winter, whenever seed is abundant. It nests high above the ground, building a neat nest of twigs and plant fibers lined with moss and lichen which holds 3–5 bluish eggs with brown spots at the rounded end. These are incubated by the female for 2 weeks and the young birds leave the nest 15–17 days after hatching. Young birds are fed immediately upon pine seeds. A nomadic bird, its numbers are difficult to establish, but in some areas it appears to be in decline due to competition with red squirrels.

Size 6¼ inches
Description Stocky body, short forked tail, large crossed bill. Male has mottled red head and body with blackish wings and tail. Female has gray plumage, darker wings, dull yellow crown and rump
Habitat Prefers mature coniferous woodland
Similar Species White-winged Crossbill has white wing bars and larger crossed bill

AMERICAN GOLDFINCH (CARDUELIS TRISTIS)

SIZE 5 inches

DESCRIPTION Small, stocky body, short forked tail, short rounded wings, large orange bill. Male is bright yellow with black forehead, white rump and undertail feathers, black wings with white bars and yellow shoulders. Black tail with white edges. Female and winter male dull olive above, yellow below, blackish wings and pale wing bars, white undertail

HABITAT Open country, weedy fields, and orchards, suburbs

SIMILAR SPECIES Breeding male distinctive. Female Lesser Goldfinch lacks white undertail

Common across most of North America with the exception of the far north, the American Goldfinch is a familiar visitor to bird feeders with its striking plumage. It is gregarious and will often mix with other birds in large feeding flocks. It breeds relatively late in the year, building a small tightly woven cup nest of grass and plant fibers high in a bush or tree. This holds 3–6 plain blue-white eggs which are incubated by the female for 2 weeks. The young can fend for themselves 12–17 days later and juvenile birds are brownish with dark wings and tail. It eats mainly seeds, but will also eat berries and insects. It shows a particular fondness for thistles, which it eats and uses to line its nest.

(PASSER DOMESTICUS) HOUSE SPARROW

The House Sparrow was introduced to the United States from the Old World in the mid-19th century and since then their numbers have dramatically increased. It is now found across much of North America, where in some areas it is considered a pest for driving out native birds. Its success is partly related to its ability to adapt to human-modified and urban environments. It nests in any available cavity, in a tree or building, lining the hole with grass or straw and laying 5–6 pale greenish-white eggs with brown-gray speckles. The female bird incubates these for 2 weeks and the young are ready to leave 2–3 weeks after hatching, when the female will then produce a second brood. It eats a variety of food, from insects and spiders to seeds, berries, grain, and bread crumbs.

SIZE 6¼ inches

DESCRIPTION Small, plump body, round head, short wings and tail, short thick bill. Upperparts are brown with dark streaks on back and wings. Male has gray crown, chestnut nape, white face and large black bib. Underparts are gray. Female has brown crown and buffy underparts

HABITAT Cultivated land and urban areas, parks, gardens, hedges

SIMILAR SPECIES Native sparrows have longer legs and thinner bill

INDEX OF COMMON NAMES

A

Anhinga	35
Avocet, American	103

B

Bittern, American	39
Blackbird, Brewer's	245
Red-winged	241
Bluebird , Mountain	199
Eastern	201
Bobolink	242
Bobwhite Northern	92
Booby, Masked	25
Bunting, Indigo	235
Painted	233
Snow	231
Bushtit	181

C

Canvasback	59
Caracara, Crested	78
Cardinal, Northern	237
Catbird, Gray	202
Chickadee, Black-capped	180
Coot, American	95
Cormorant, Double-crested	33
Great	31
Cowbird, Brown-headed	246
Crane, Sandhill	101
Creeper, Brown	186
Crossbill, Red	251
Crow, American	171
Cuckoo, Yellow-billed	125

D

Dipper, American	189
Dove, Mourning	124
Rock	123
Duck, Tufted	57
Ruddy	61
Wood	53
Dunlin	107

E

Eagle, Bald	77
Golden	75
Egret, Great	41
Eider, King	56

F

Falcon, Peregrine	83
Prairie	81
Flicker, Northern	154
Flycatcher, Least	155
Vermilion	159
Frigatebird, Magnificent	37
Fulmar, Northern	19

G

Gannet, Northern	24
Gnatcatcher, Blue-gray	190
Goldeneye, Common	60
Goldfinch, American	252
Goose, Canada	50
Snow	51
Grackle, Common	247
Grebe, Pied-billed	17
Western	18
Grosbeak, Blue	239
Evening	249
Grouse, Blue	85
Sage	87
Guillemot, Black	119
Gull, Great Black-backed	111

Gull, Herring	112
Ring-billed	113

H

Harrier, Northern	66
Hawk , Rough-legged	70
Sharp-shinned	67
Red-shouldered	71
Hawk, Red-tailed	69
Heron, Great Blue	38
Hummingbird, Calliope	147
Ruby-throated	145
Rufous	146

I

Ibis, White	43

J

Jaeger, Parasitic	110
Jay, Blue	165
Gray	166
Steller's	167
Junco, Dark-eyed	230
Yellow-eyed	229

K

Kestrel, American	79
Killdeer	99
Kingbird, Eastern	160
Kingfisher, Belted	149
Kinglet , Ruby-crowned	191
Golden-crowned	193

L

Lark, Horned	174
Loon, Common	16

M

Magpie, Black-billed	170
Mallard	54
Meadowlark, Eastern	243
Western	244
Merganser, Common	62
Merlin	80
Mockingbird, Northern	203
Moorhen, Common	98

N

Nighthawk, Common	140
Nutcracker, Clark's	169
Nuthatch, Red-breasted	185

O

Osprey	73
Owl, Barn	131
Burrowing	129
Great Gray	139
Great Horned	135
Long-eared	132
Short-eared	133
Snowy	137
Oystercatcher, American	102

P

Partridge, Gray	84
Pelican, American White	27
Brown	29
Pheasant, Ring-necked	89
Phoebe, Black	157
Pintail, Northern	55
Ptarmigan, Rock	88
Puffin, Atlantic	121
Tufted	122
Purple Gallinule	97
Purple Martin	175

Q

Quail, California	93

R

Raven, Common	173
Razorbill	118
Redstart, American	217
Roadrunner, Greater	127
Robin, American	197

S

Sandpiper, Least	106
Sapsucker, Yellow-bellied	153
Screech-owl, Eastern	136
Shearwater, Sooty	20
Shrike, Loggerhead	161
Skimmer, Black	117
Snipe, Common	109
Sparrow, American Tree	222
Chipping	221
Fox	224
House	253
Savannah	223
Song	225
White-crowned	226
Sparrow, White-throated	227
Spoonbill, Roseate	47
Starling, European	205
Stork, Wood	45
Storm-petrel, Wilson's	21
Swallow, Bank	178
Barn	179
Tree	177
Swan, Trumpeter	49
Tundra	48
Swift, Chimney	143

T

Tanager, Scarlet	219
Tern, Black	115
Tern, Common	114
Thrasher, Brown	204
Thrush, Hermit	198
Varied	195
Titmouse, Tufted	183
Towhee, Eastern	220
Tropicbird, White-tailed	23
Turkey, Wild	91

V

Vireo, Red-eyed	163
Vireo, Yellow-throated	162
Vulture, Black	63
Turkey	65

W

Warbler, Black-and-white	214
Blackburnian	210
Magnolia	213
Yellow	209
Yellow-rumped	211
Waxwing, Bohemian	208
Cedar	207
Whip-poor-will	141
Willet	105
Woodpecker, Downy	149
Hairy	151
Red-headed	152
Wood-Pewee, Western	156
Wren, House	187
Winter	188

Y

Yellowlegs, Greater	104
Yellowthroat, Common	215

INDEX OF SCIENTIFIC NAMES

A

Accipiter striatus	67
Aechmophorus occidentalis	18
Agelaius phoeniceus	241
Aix sponsa	53
Ajaia ajaja	47
Alca torda	118
Anas acuta	55
platyrhynchos	54
Anhinga anhinga	35
Aquila chrysaetos	75
Archilochus colubris	145
Ardea herodias	38
alba	41
Asio flammeus	133
otus	132
Aythya fuligula	57
Aythya valisineria	59

B

Bombycilla cedrorum	207
garrulus	208
Botaurus lentiginosus	39
Branta canadensis	50
Bubo virginianus	135
Bucephala clangula	60
Buteo jamaicensis	69
lagopus	70
lineatus	71

C

Calidris alpina	107
minutilla	106
Callipepla californica	93
Caprimulgus vociferus	141
Caracara plancus	78
Cardinalis cardinalis	237
Carduelis tristis	252
Cathartes aura	65
Catharus guttatus	198
Catoptrophorus semipalmatus	105
Centrocercus urophasianus	87
Cepphus grylle	119
Certhia americana	186
Ceryle alcyon	148
Chaetura pelagica	143
Charadrius vociferus	99
Chen caerulescens	51
Chlidonias niger	115
Chordeiles minor	140
Cinclus mexicanus	189
Circus cyaneus	66
Coccothraustes vespertinus	249
Coccyzus americanus	125
Colaptes auratus	154
Colinus virginianus	92
Columba livia	123
Contopus sordidulus	156
Coragyps atratus	63
Corvus brachyrhynchos	171
corax	173
Cyanocitta cristata	165
stelleri	167
Cygnus buccinator	49
columbianus	48

D

Dendragapus obscurus	85
Dendroica coronata	211
Dendroica fusca	208
magnolia	213

petechia	209
Dolichonyx oryzivorus	242
Dumetella carolinensis	202

E

Empidonax minimus	155
Eremophila alpestris	174
Eudocimus albus	43
Euphagus cyanocephalus	245

F

Falco columbarius	80
mexicanus	81
peregrinus	83
sparverius	79
Fratercula arctica	121
cirrhata	122
Fregata magnificens	37
Fulica americana	95
Fulmarus glacialis	19

G

Gallinago gallinago	109
Gallinula chloropus	98
Gavia immer	16
Geococcyx californianus	127
Geothlypis trichas	215
Grus canadensis	101
Guiraca caerulea	239

H

Haematopus palliatus	102
Haliaeetus leucocephalus	77
Hirundo rustica	179

I

Ixoreus naevius	195

J

Junco hyemalis	230
phaeonotus	229

L

Lagopus mutus	88
Lanius ludovicianus	161
Larus argentatus	112
delawarensis	113
marinus	111
Loxia curvirostra	251

M

Melanerpes erythrocephalus	152
Meleagris gallopavo	91
Melospiza melodia	225
Mergus merganser	62
Mimus polyglottos	203
Mniotilta varia	214
Molothrus ater	246
Morus bassanus	22
Mycteria americana	45

N

Nucifraga columbiana	169
Nyctea scandiaca	137

O

Oceanites oceanicus	21
Otus asio	136
Oxyura jamaicensis	61

P

Pandion haliaetus	73
Parus atricapillus	180
bicolor	183
Passer domesticus	253
Passerculus sandwichensis	223
Passerella iliaca	224
Passerina ciris	233
cyanea	235

Pelecanus erythrorhynchos	27
occidentalis	29
Perdix perdix	84
Perisoreus canadensis	166
Phaethon lepturus	23
Phalacrocorax auritus	33
carbo	31
Phasianus colchicus	89
Pica pica	170
Picoides pubescens	149
villosus	151
Pipilo erythrophthalmus	220
Piranga olivacea	219
Plectrophenax nivalis	231
Podilymbus podiceps	17
Polioptila caerulea	190
Porphyrula martinica	97
Progne subis	175
Psaltriparus minimus	181
Puffinus griseus	20
Pyrocephalus rubinus	159

Q

Quiscalus quiscula	247

R

Recurvirostra americana	103
Regulus calendula	191
Regulus satrapa	193
riparia	178

S

Sayornis nigricans	157
Selasphorus rufus	146
Setophaga ruticilla	217
Sialia currucoides	199
sialis	201
Sitta canadensis	185
Somateria spectabilis	56
Speotyto cunicularia	129
Sphyrapicus varius	153
Spizella arborea	222
passerina	221
Stellula calliope	147
Stercorarius parasiticus	110
Sterna hirundo	114
Strix nebulosa	139
Sturnella magna	243
neglecta	244
Sturnus vulgaris	205
Sula dactylatra	25

T

Tachycineta bicolor	177
Toxostoma rufum	204
Tringa melanoleuca	104
Troglodytes aedon	187
troglodytes	188
Turdus migratorius	197
Tyrannus tyrannus	160
Tyto alba	131

V

Vireo flavifrons	162
olivaceus	163

Z

Zenaida macroura	124
Zonotrichia albicollis	227
leucophrys	226

PICTURE ACKNOWLEDGMENTS

The publisher would like to thank Photolibrary.com for providing the photographs for this book. We would also like to thank the following for their kind permission to reproduce their photographs:

Adam Jones 92; Alain Christof 73; Alan G Nelson 33, 67, 147, 151, 252; Ben Osbourne 65; Bob Bennett 27, 45 ; Bob Rozinski 109; Breck P Kent 154, 171; Brian Milne 56; C M Perrings 119, 159; Charles Palek 161; Chris Knights 57; Chris Sharp 225; Dale & Marian Zimmerman 156; Daniel J Cox 50, 226, 227; David Tipling 14/15, 71, 88, 205; Dennis Green 80, 115, 133, 188; Dieter & Mary Plage 87; Don Enger 18; Don Hadden/Ardea 20; Doug Allan 21; Edward Robinson 47; Eric Woods 55; Eyal Barton 70; Frank Huber 38; Frank Schneidermeyer 53, 61, 91, 117, 220, 244, 241; Fred Unverhau 141; G A Maclean 178; Geoff Kidd 9 ; Hans Reinhard 251, 253; Henry R Fox 59; Jack Dermid 124; James Robinson 127, 189; Jim Zipp/Ardea, London 174; Joe Mcdonald 113, 229, 160; John Anderson 181; John Gerlach 51, 103, 153, 185, 217, 242, 249; John Harris 24 ; John Netherton 136; John S Dunning 162; Ken Cole 177, 180; Kenneth Day 30, 209; Konrad Wothe 6; Len Rue 167; Lon E Lauber 77, 79; Manfred Pfefferle 114; Maresa Pryor 78; Marie Read 29, 215; Mario Deeble & Victoria Stone 31; Mark A Chappell 122; Mark Hamblin 60, 66, 83, 112, 121, 131, 135, 170, 208; Matthias Breiter 85; Maurice Tibbles 37; Max Gibbs 23; Michael Habicht 195, 224; Michael Leach 132, 137; Mike Price 165; N V Howell 183; Niall Benvie 75, 187; Norbert Rosing 48; Patti Murray 210; Philippe Henry 139; Richard Day 101, 125, 143, 148, 149, 152, 191, 197, 199, 211, 239, 247; Richard Packwood 19, 54, 89, 111, 118, 173, 246; Robert Lubeck 213, 214; Roger Aitkinhead 93; Ron Willocks 140; Scott Smith 186; Stan Osolinski 17, 25, 32, 35, 39, 41, 49, 63, 95, 97, 99, 105, 123, 129, 166, 202, 203, 245; Steve Turner 81; T C Nature 190, 193; Ted Levin 155; Terry Andrewartha 84, 106, 179, 222; Tom Edwards 219; Tom Leach 104, 110, 231; Tom Ulrich 16, 24 69, 102, 145, 146, 157, 163, 169, 175, 198, 201, 204, 207, 221, 223, 233, 237; Tony Tilford 107, 230, 235

Cover images:

Top from left to right: Tom Edwards; Mark A Chappell; Mark Hamblin

Bottom from left to right: Wendell Metzen/Getty Images; John Harris